W9-AYO-642

11/06

THE BRUMBACK LIBRARY
OF VAN WERT COUNTY
VAN WERT, OHIO

CB

THE
IQ
ANSWER

Also by Dr. Frank Lawlis

The ADD Answer

THE
IQ
ANSWER

MAXIMIZING YOUR CHILD'S POTENTIAL

DR. FRANK LAWLIS

VIKING

VIKING
Published by the Penguin Group
Penguin Group (USA) Inc., 375 Hudson Street,
New York, New York 10014, U.S.A.
Penguin Group (Canada), 90 Eglinton Avenue East, Suite 700, Toronto,
Ontario, Canada M4P 2Y3 (a division of Pearson Penguin Canada Inc.)
Penguin Books Ltd, 80 Strand, London WC2R 0RL, England
Penguin Ireland, 25 St. Stephen's Green, Dublin 2, Ireland
(a division of Penguin Books Ltd)
Penguin Books Australia Ltd, 250 Camberwell Road, Camberwell,
Victoria 3124, Australia (a division of Pearson Australia Group Pty Ltd)
Penguin Books India Pvt Ltd, 11 Community Centre,
Panchsheel Park, New Delhi – 110 017, India
Penguin Group (NZ), Cnr Airborne and Rosedale Roads, Albany,
Auckland 1310, New Zealand (a division of Pearson New Zealand Ltd)
Penguin Books (South Africa) (Pty) Ltd, 24 Sturdee Avenue,
Rosebank, Johannesburg 2196, South Africa

Penguin Books Ltd, Registered Offices: 80 Strand, London WC2R 0RL, England

First published in 2006 by Viking Penguin, a member of Penguin Group (USA) Inc.

1   3   5   7   9   10   8   6   4   2

Copyright © Frank Lawlis, 2006
All rights reserved

ISBN 0-670-03784-2

Printed in the United States of America
Set in Granjon
Designed by Level C

Dedicated to my children, T. Frank, Luci, and Erica, for their enduring love and courage, and the supreme happiness I have been blessed with for their being on this earth with me.

Each has been a major part of my reason for being in a global and individual way.

PREFACE

The success of *The ADD Answer* overwhelmed me with letters of gratitude and hope from parents of children with ADD and adults who suffer from the concentration problems of attention deficit disorder. Gratifying as it was, there remained a large number of people who wrote and asked about other issues, like depression and anxiety, especially obsessive disorders that could have alternative solutions. Even more interesting was the huge interest from executives who wanted a step toward success on their career ladders, and from law students and medical hopefuls who had failed their qualifying tests and were desperate to pass to the next level. This book concerns these areas left unnoticed.

There are answers that will go beyond your imagination in discovering the potential within your tremendous brain power. Many of us have heard the old saying that you only use 10 percent of your brain, which is not true. What is true is that you have the capacity to make your brain 900 percent more available through the exercises and methods explained in this book. The process is called *neuroplasticity,* and is defined by your brain's ability to mold itself around most needs you have confronting you. This process does not happen instantaneously, but it does occur with amazing speed. I have seen people with major strokes that left them without the ability to speak or walk regain these capacities and more. I have seen people curled up in helpless fetal positions and in comas who have started new lives. I have seen people with diseases that are thought to be incurable healed through these basic approaches.

But these techniques are also intended for the normal to become supernormal. Forty drug companies are putting tremendous financial investments into new brain-boosting formulations to resist the onslaught of

Alzheimer's and Parkinson's diseases, but these drugs also carry the potential to allow all of us take the next step into our capabilities and into the super-brain generation. Some drugs are in clinical trials already, raising concerns about the idea of having "steroid brains."

We already know the techniques for great mind development. Let me share a letter from a guest I saw on *Dr. Phil.*

> *Dr. Lawlis,*
>
> *I just wanted to let you know that thanks to the techniques you showed Justin during the short amount of time he spent with you last year in Los Angeles, Justin got his report card this week and has A's in every subject (except Music—the boy can't sing but does well in the theory part). He is so much happier and is looking forward to his final year in middle school.*
>
> *He's actually talking already about trying to enter the Baccalaureate program at a local high school. This program, if successfully completed, gives you University credits but you must maintain an average of 85% in English, Math, Science and whatever electives you take.*
>
> *He has changed so much it's incredible. In large part, he uses the techniques you showed him and it is working well which has increased his self-confidence. He was the top achiever in his class this year and has been invited to assist his current teacher with a presentation at a conference for Exceptional Children in October 2005. The changes since 2004 are incredible and it's a long way from when I had to talk him into going to school most every morning.*
>
> *Thank you again!! It is so wonderful for us that we had the opportunity to meet you and benefit from your expertise. Pass my thanks on to Dr. Phil because in the end we never would have had this opportunity without him and his show.*
>

Sincerely,
Lucie Thomas

As in all my books, examples from my personal experience are part of my approach. You will read that I was diagnosed as mentally retarded as an infant and certainly had some problems cognitively. Maybe I am still retarded, and maybe mental retardation is a permanent barrier to some, but maybe not. Maybe we Forrest Gumps have some special contribution that surpasses the usual academic measures of intelligence. Albert Einstein, Thomas Edison, Bill Gates, just to name a few, would agree. Who knows the extent of the human brain or the human spirit?

I wrote this book with the conscious mission to offer action steps for achieving greater intellectual capacities regardless of where you are or have been. I could talk in abstract terms, but, being an ex-coach, I prefer to put verbs in my sentences that give very real promises. And I give my promise that you can raise your IQ at least five, maybe ten or twenty, points after you read this book and find the action plan that works for you. You can succeed in anything you can imagine, but you have to invest in that plan with your heart and mind. God gave you this precious treasure of free will and the freedom to be something greater than you are. To accomplish this goal, you need to truly believe and open yourself to the challenges that await you on your path. It is often said that you only get out of something what you put into it. This book is not about cheer-leading you into a better frame of mind so you will be more motivated— you have to believe in yourself.

This book explains how your brain, mind, and soul work together. It is like having a motor with three functions—fuel and air mixture, electrical spark, and pistons and valves—all acting together. If you have problems in one area, the engine won't work. I can show you how to make all the parts work so you can use your unique power to get to where you want to go.

So how do you discover your fullest potential and begin to apply it? You must have the resources, the skills, and the methods to utilize the power within. You must also recognize the patience that is required to put this new wisdom to use. That is the purpose of this book: to give you direction so that you can achieve all for which you were destined. This is the blueprint for your path toward achieving everything that God wants for you.

YOUR INTELLECTUAL IQ

One look at a brain scan will help anyone understand the power of mindful breathing. For example, just by breathing in certain patterns, parts of the brain begin to glow with power, indicating an increase of activity. ADD sufferers experience some of the most dramatic changes to the brain. In chapter 2, "The Breathing Brain," I will outline some of these processes, and suggest breathing exercises to address specific problems.

Chapter 3, "Brain Detoxification," discusses toxins in the environment that compromise intellectual power. It is virtually impossible for a race car to reach its highest speeds without a clean engine and fresh oil. It is even more so with human capacities. If you're exposed to any one of the dozens of poisons in the environment, you must detoxify your brain. This chapter gives a step-by-step program for restoring your brain to its greatest vitality.

Chapter 4, "Nurturing Your Intellect Through Brain Fuel," talks about specific lifestyle choices you can make to actually get smarter—nutrition, exercise, sleep patterns—along with daily plans for accomplishing these goals. Using the metaphor of a carburetor, the brain needs a fuel mixture of air and food. The important factors are how to get enough fresh air and what kinds of foods nurture the brain to its ultimate power. In addition, I'll show how sound sleep patterns naturally restore good mental health. This does not mean medicated sleep, however, because medicinal sleep aids do not lead to complete restoration.

Physical and mental exercises make a huge difference in the way your brain works. Special exercises correspond to specific portions of the brain, such as the cerebellum (which controls balance and focus), and the temporal (memory) and frontal (organizational abilities) areas of the brain. This chapter also covers specific goals, such as increased memory and lowered anxiety.

Chapter 5, "The Foggy Mind," illustrates how the environment can play a negative role in maximizing your brainpower. It is to your advantage to be aware of these toxic elements because they can destroy your life, yet they can be eliminated with little time or expense.

YOUR EMOTIONAL IQ

Too often our emotional energy is drained away by the noise and distractions of worry and fear. Used by all the sages of the world, the steps toward achieving a sense of peace and harmony are essential to emotional well-being, something that we all can accomplish. Chapter 6,

"Restoring Your Brainpower," gives steps for overcoming worry, fear, and anxiety that detract from emotional genius.

All great inventors, writers, artists, and super-successful businesspeople admit that their sources for inspiration do not come from their skills in problem solving, but from a central core of creativity that comes to them through their unconsciousness and expresses itself through their own understanding and language. This source has been described by philosophers and shamans for centuries, yet remains a secret even to those who already have the skills to gain this powerful ally. Through discussions of imagery and the knowledge of symbols, chapter 7, "The Six Faces of Genius," describes these skills in order to help you create new and more effective solutions to the problems you face at work and at home.

Beginning with the way we are taught to think by our parents and later by society or trillion-dollar advertising efforts, we learn to process information in ways that can lead us to anxiety and depression. How many people believe that skinny bodies are more attractive than curvy ones? How many of us can go through a day without feeling guilty? These self-destructive thought patterns also imprison us in a revolving cycle of self-deprecation and ultimately diminish our inner genius. Chapter 8, "Overcoming the Emotional Traps That Drain Your Genius," says it is time to free yourself; enormous energies will emerge in the wake of happiness. These rewards are there for you, so open the doors.

Our emotional peace relies on our internal thinking structure. We are our own worst enemies when we meet internal conflict. By correcting wrong thinking patterns, you are free to accomplish tremendous goals in all areas of your life. Assessments and steps for achieving rational, realistic, and positive thought patterns are outlined in chapter 9, "Right Thinking." When practiced and reinforced, right thinking gives you the emotional power to be all that you can be.

Lots of motivational books will tell you only how you can improve your own life, but that is almost an exercise in futility. You are not born alone in this world and certainly do not live completely without social influences. One of the deepest needs in a human being is to relate to other human beings and gain support from them. This social power can take strength away from you or give you new ways to develop greater self-confidence. Chapter 10, "Interpersonal Empowerment," offers you those specific steps in empowering yourself through interpersonal relationships.

YOUR CREATIVE IQ

Chapter 11, "Raising the Limits of Your Creativity," discusses the nuts and bolts of creativity—how the brains of creative people appear to be more open to incoming stimuli from the surrounding environment, whereas other people's brains might shut out this same information. Creative people maintain contact with this extra information constantly streaming in from the environment and are therefore more open to new possibilities.

It is a well-documented fact that when you utilize the mental energies of those around you, there is an important surge of powerful creative processing. This is the basic reason why successful leaders surround themselves with innovators. Whether it is family or colleagues, you can do the same. Chapter 12, "Smart Love," will outline how to use the unique resources of your personal support network to give your own creativity and confidence a boost. Chapter 13, "Raising a Family or a Nation to Full Potential," shows the broader application of these ideas.

NOTES ON THE GENIUS WITHIN US

Within each of us is a powerful source of wisdom, passed down through our ancestry and experiences. These insights are difficult to understand because they are usually masked in our dreams and intuitions. Unlocking those very wise sources can be fairly simple yet yield profound results. Using imagery and the common knowledge of symbols, we can learn what these deep thoughts are and how to discover their powerful applications for tremendous insight into obstacles and challenges. Great leaders and inventors in the history of the world used these same methods. The wisdom you discover within yourself will give you genius insight into yourself and others, giving you greater perspective and opportunity.

ACKNOWLEDGMENTS

It would be impossible to fully acknowledge the contribution that Phil McGraw (Dr. Phil) has made to this book from its conception to reality. Our kinship is based on more than thirty-five years of working in a partnership in which we have each had to trust our professional life to the other's integrity as a friend and professional colleague in many memorable projects. He has always shown me honest support and enthusiastic feedback for my dreams, and whatever success I have enjoyed is rooted in his generosity and encouragement. This book is only the most recent endeavor in which we share a mission to serve the public with important information that has the potential of changing people's lives.

Jan Miller, my literary agent and amazing friend, has been my greatest guide with his profound insight and advice. Both he and my agent, Shannon Miser-Marven, have worked tirelessly in my professional development as a writer and teacher. I would be lost in this maze of publication business without them.

Dr. Maggie Robinson, a major league writer of health books in her own right, has always offered me the opportunity to share my thoughts and concepts in words with open enthusiasm and loving criticism. She is always positive as well as wise in her appraisal of my attempts to convey my half-baked ideas into full-blown usable concepts, and I am grateful for our relationship.

The genius behind the wordsmithing in my books has been Wes Smith, a total mastermind in grasping my awkward sentences and making them understandable. His wit and expertise are major blessings for my attempts to share my on-the-edge ideas with readers.

I am especially appreciative of American Mensa and Pam Donahoo,

CAE, for the incredible association we have had over the last three years. Being the supervisory psychologist for Mensa has been important for my professional interest in human intelligence, but the emotional connections I've had with this organization have created a close relationship that I have cherished in my personal life.

I have to thank Nancy Autin, my sister and lifelong best friend, not only for reading and critiquing the manuscript and evaluating its content based on her thirty-eight years as a school counselor and teacher, but also for the open love always available to me. Also playing major, multiple roles in my personal and professional relationships is my partner in the Lawlis and Peavey Centers for Psychoneurological Change, its CEO, Dr. Barbara Peavey. Dr. Peavey has supported this endeavor with her insightful applications of the concepts formulated in this book, making them real and even practical.

CONTENTS

THE
IQ
ANSWER

One

YOU ARE ENOUGH

Your mind is perhaps the least understood but most critical aspect of your existence. It is much more than the body's computer or center of intelligence. It is the locus of passion and joy. It is home to that distinctly human quality, your self-awareness, and it is probably also the seat of our unique spirituality, the soul.

I am writing this book to help you better understand your mind, its functions, and what it needs to operate at its full potential. I promise that once you have a better grasp of these things, you will be able to operate at higher intellectual levels for longer periods so that you create far greater opportunities and more joy in your life.

You are already equipped with everything you need to perform at higher levels of achievement. The answers, as they say, "are all in your head." I am concerned that many people don't reach their full potential for success and fulfillment because their brains aren't functioning at their highest levels. Physical or psychological trauma can affect your brain functions in ways that are difficult to detect, yet highly detrimental. I will provide information and prescriptive step-by-step advice to help you evaluate whether your brain is functioning at its full potential. Then I will give you the tools you need to "fine tune" the incredible engine that drives your intellect, your reasoning, your self-awareness, and the very essence of what makes you human.

Many of you may know of my involvement as chief content adviser for the television show *Dr. Phil*. In that role, I am very involved in analyzing the guests and the stories they tell on the show. I will share with you some of those stories, as well as other behind-the-scenes occurrences that don't get on the air because of time considerations, scheduling complexities, or simply because they unfold outside of camera range.

One of those intriguing stories came from Mark, a thirty-five-year-old executive of a software company. At the age of eleven, Mark was injured in an automobile crash. A drunk driver ran a stop sign while traveling at more than seventy miles per hour and broadsided the small family car in which Mark was a passenger. His mother was killed instantly, and his left leg and hip were crushed.

Infants born to women who developed post-traumatic stress disorder during pregnancy have, as their mothers do, unusually low concentrations of the hormone cortisol, which might partially explain why these children tend to develop ADD symptoms. (*Endocrinology*, July 2005)

After many surgeries and a very painful rehabilitation, Mark regained his mobility. In fact, he became a top swimmer in high school and college. Mark had heroic levels of discipline and motivation that led to his athletic accomplishments. He applied those same traits to his schoolwork, but without the same level of results. He was a poor student, earning a C average throughout high school and community college. He struggled to remain academically eligible for sports. The motivation was always present, but he had difficulties in focusing his attention and with memorization tasks. He failed history and algebra classes in two out of six terms.

Mark's high school friends consisted of three close buddies who had reputations as "probable dropouts," which they lived up to by the time they were sixteen. This would have been Mark's fate as well, had it not been for his continued interest in sports. He was mostly a loner at the community college he attended, but received strong moral support from Mary, whom he married after four dates.

Mary was Mark's salvation academically. She took the same computer classes so she could tutor him through many sleepless nights, helping him pass the tests. Still, he struggled academically, and their marriage failed. Their divorce and his struggle to graduate from college finally led Mark to seek help. He'd come to suspect that he had ADHD (attention deficit hyperactivity disorder). I reviewed Mark's case as a potential segment for *Dr. Phil* and I was struck by his remarkable story and the predictable shutdown I had witnessed in other similar cases. Mark did not have ADHD. But his brain had been impacted in a way that produced similar symptoms. Remember, this was a very determined young athlete who was strong both physically and mentally. He was severely injured in the car accident that occurred when he was eleven, and doctors at the time could not give him the typical painkillers because of his age and the risk of addiction. So Mark used his considerable discipline and determination to shut down pain's path through his brain and body. He found that he could dissociate mentally, placing his mind in another reality to shut out the pain. It was a remarkable mental feat, really. He later tapped that same mental strength as a competitive swimmer.

Ironically, Mark's conquest of pain through mind control led to his athletic success, but it was probably the source of both his academic and emotional difficulties. To endure the pain of his accident injuries, Mark had taught himself to dissociate from anything that caused physical or emotional discomfort. He could throw the switch and refocus his mind on other matters. Unfortunately, it became akin to a reflexive action, so that whenever there was a mental or emotional challenge, his mind redirected its focus automatically.

He provided clues to this when he told me about his failed marriage: "I just was so shut down; I could not tell Mary what was going on inside me. I knew I needed to be more honest, but I felt physical pain when I thought about telling her that she was married to a failure, a desperate loser. I just dissociated into living another person's life, a person who did not care. I don't blame her for giving up on me."

Therapy for Mark began with dancing and martial arts, exercises to stimulate the brain and creativity. He learned special breathing techniques and relaxation thorough biofeedback. He was also counseled so that he learned to break through the walls of self-deception. He discovered that the fear and depression that had accompanied his physical pain were blocking him from using his mind to its greatest potential and he learned healthier coping strategies.

Once he mastered all the breathing techniques and relaxation, Mark began to reap huge rewards. His attention span and his ability to memorize improved dramatically and his performance in school followed suit.

Perhaps most important, Mark's "emotional intelligence" soared: he regained his self-confidence and an optimistic view of life. Within a year he graduated from college, developed his own computer software company, and reignited his relationship with his ex-wife.

Annie brought another story of unrealized potential to us for consideration. She had been sexually abused by her uncle from age eight to eleven. Although there was no penetration, the uncle would rub his body on hers and tell her what a bad girl she was for making him excited. Annie was just a child, so she accepted that she was responsible for her uncle's perversion. She came to believe that she was evil. As you can imagine, her relationships suffered. After multiple marriages to men who exploited her poor self-image, she found herself on welfare with two children. But, perhaps by fate, she met a psychologist who helped her understand and overcome her negative self-image and her relationship problems.

Post-traumatic stress disorder affects at least 5 percent of the American population and is the fastest growing disability, according to the Department of Veterans Affairs. (Associated Press, 2005)

Annie's uncle had stunted her development, emotionally and mentally. Her therapy brought her up to mature levels and opened the full flow of energy to her mind. She discovered that she had a very superior IQ. As her self-confidence and optimism about the future increased, Annie was able to tap into the full power of her brain for the first time in her life. She went to law school, graduated, and became a prominent attorney who specializes in cases involving the abuse of women.

NEUROPLASTICITY: NEGATIVE AND POSITIVE SHIFTS IN THE BRAIN

Mark and Annie both possessed strong intellects and great willpower. When they experienced childhood trauma, they instinctively rewired their brains so that they could cope with the physical and psychic pain. This process of rewiring the brain is known as *neuroplasticity*. It isn't just a psychological process; it actually occurs at the cellular level so that it is both biological and neurological. And as you can imagine, it creates all sorts of chaos for those who experience it.

This rewiring alters the brain's interconnections, causing reductions in the input it can absorb and, in turn, limiting our options for response. If you've ever had the frustration of having a computer switch itself to "safe mode," then you have a sense of what this is like. The computer still can perform basic functions in this protective mode, but cannot perform more advanced functions.

Much the same thing happens to the brain when we are traumatized as Mark and Annie were. They shut down their connection to physical and psychic pain, but in this mental "safe mode," which is the "lite" version of a coma, they also lost the capacity for joy and optimism, and along with them, the full power of their intellects. Fortunately, there are ways to switch your brain out of safe mode, just as you can do with your computer—if you have the necessary skills or access to expertise.

Alicia Townsend demonstrated this phenomenon in her dissertation at the University of North Texas when she completed QEEG (quantitative electroencephalogram) brain maps of adults who were sexually abused as children. She found poorer coherence (neurological transmissions across the brain), general slowing of brain activity, and less alpha activity (relaxation and comfort) than average brains without trauma. Moreover, there were higher indications of cortisol, which is a natural neurotoxin. These findings support the idea that psychological trauma can affect our biology and the way our brains function for the rest of our lives.

Psychological traumas, like those experienced by Mark and Annie, have been the subject of extensive research. A recent survey supported by the National Institute of Mental Health found that approximately one half of the population suffers at least one traumatic emotional insult by the age of fourteen. Few of these individuals seek medical treatment. The most common disorders that result are depression, anxiety, and phobias.

I have had many patients with stories similar to those of Mark and Annie, and my career has been dedicated to understanding the impact of physical and psychological trauma. I know the most effective ways to rehabilitate those who've suffered mental insults. There are three basic steps:

1. Restart the brain's power.

2. Eliminate emotional obstacles.

3. Tap into the mind's true potential and ignite creativity to open new opportunities.

Do you ever wonder why many well-intentioned programs like Head Start and many missionary programs have such limited measurable success? Have you wondered why psychotherapy approaches work about 50 percent of the time at best? Drug rehabilitation programs are successful only about 10 to 15 percent of the time. The reason is that these programs do not address the potential environmental or emotional blocks that can limit brain function. We need to start with a "conditioning fitness program for the brain" before we assume rational learning can take place. Too often, our minds are operating at less than full capacity. To return to the car analogy, it is like trying to climb a mountain with only four of the six cylinders functioning. No matter how much fuel you pump to the damaged engine, it isn't going to be able to give you full power. It's the same with a brain that has undergone some sort of insult or rewiring.

You have to tap your full potential neurologically before you have the power to run up whatever mountains you seek to scale. If your mind is being drained of its power by emotional stunting or crippling coping mechanisms, it is all but impossible to function at your optimum levels.

Anyone who has endured violence, sexual abuse, severe injury, or dysfunctional relationships likely has suffered some level of neurological insult. More than 25 percent of women in the United States suffer some form of abuse in their lifetimes. Students who have been stigmatized socially by their physical or mental labels deal with enormous stress, anxiety, and depression during their school experiences. Several children have been diagnosed with post-traumatic stress disorder after receiving hostile or judgmental treatment from teachers during this most sensitive of times. Those who already have a reduced mental function are the most vulnerable to further debilitation. Attention deficit disorder, obsessive disorders, learning disorders, and other psychological barriers make it all the more difficult to keep the brain functioning at optimum levels mentally and emotionally. Those who are suffering from such disorders can lose even more mental capacity with the slightest stress to the brain because their defenses are already down. A simple negative comment from a family member, classmate, teacher, or coach at a critical point in development can send sensitive young people reeling. Sadly, far too many people do not realize that while they cannot control the external things that happen to them, they do have control over how they respond internally. The damage that we do to ourselves is often far greater than what others do to us.

The brain's "safe mode" is nature's way of protecting your mind in times of high stress. It is not designed to be a permanent condition that prevents you from being the creative, joyous, adventurous, intelligent person you were meant to be. When your mind is not at full power, not only are you more vulnerable, you are less capable of finding solutions to your problems. So problems tend to build upon each other. Phobias and nightmares lead to obsessive behavior, paranoia, and depression because your mind can't fight back. Relationship problems escalate because you can't create the internal dialogue needed to resolve conflicts and control offensive behaviors. Often, people forfeit responsibility for their actions by claiming the victim's role, which only sends them into a deeper downward spiral. They continue to make poor choices and bad decisions regarding mates, jobs, money, drugs, and alcohol.

Does this sound like you? If you feel your life is spiraling downward, caught in a trap or mired in mud, there is a very strong likelihood that for some reason, your mind is not operating at its optimum levels. The feeling of being trapped or stuck indicates that your brain patterns are stuck in a loop so that you repeat the same unproductive behaviors over and over again—with the same sad results. No one wants to live that way. But too often, those who are not at full mental strength can't see a way out.

Barbara was the terror of my psychological ward early in my career. I was the last of many who had evaluated her to see if any therapy might be helpful. A drug addict, she was in a trap of self-denial and fear. Yet there were signs of strength and determination that gave me cause to think she might respond to therapy. She had a rebellious spirit, so I asked her to join me in a conspiracy. I told her that I believed she was a lot smarter than any of the other doctors thought possible. She agreed to let me test her after I promised to show her the results before I told anyone else. Previous evaluations had been written in such a muddle of psychological jargon that even I had a hard time understanding the diagnosis.

When Barbara showed up the next day I told her that her scientific diagnosis was "disagreeable nag."

"You will probably end up alone and friendless," I said.

She was appalled.

I told her that she was in the "More-So Trap," in which people don't change their self-destructive ways, they just get "more so."

Then I told her that there was hope for her. My message to her was the same that this book offers you. We all have the power to change within ourselves. Barbara's label was "addict." But it was just a label stuck on her by someone else. It was a description, not a cause, and not a death sentence either. She did not have to accept that label. She could reject it and create her own reality.

Barbara returned to my office three more times to see if I had changed my diagnosis. Finally she said she was ready to rip off the label. She agreed to follow my three-faceted plan. And just as I suspected, she had the strength of will to change the course of her life. She defied those who had predicted that she would never recover from her addicted past. She cleared out the cobwebs, cranked her brain up to unprecedented levels, and became one of the most creative and productive artists in her community.

> Over forty drug companies "are pursuing . . . the holy grail of pharmacology, a pill to boost sagging memory—Viagra for the brain." ("The Quest for a Smart Pill," *Popular Science*, September 2005)

THE OTHER SIDE OF DEVELOPMENT: THE GOLDEN YEARS

The trauma of insult to the brain can have a major impact on all ranges of development, but the elderly are particularly vulnerable. Of course, by society's standards, I qualify as elderly now so I am sensitive to this fact. Sadly, I've seen firsthand that unless people of my generation take care of our bodies and minds, we risk tumbling down a slippery slope toward dementia. The epidemic of Alzheimer's and Parkinson's diseases will place greater stress on society unless we adopt the preventive health measures offered in the pages that follow. If you worry about becoming a burden to your family in this regard, I have included material that will give you comfort as well as access to continued productivity—and joy—in the years to come.

Besides my own health, I have an additional personal investment in and awareness of this issue. My mother was diagnosed with fronto-temporal dementia (FTD), a terminal illness with a more destructive process than Alzheimer's. Her suffering was one of the most difficult things I've experienced, but I am hoping that what I learned and drew from this tragedy will benefit many, many people by saving them from a similar, horrific fate.

ASSESSING YOUR OWN BRAINPOWER

What are your plans for the future? Are you stuck? Do you still dream of getting a college degree, professional certificate, or license of some kind? Do you want a better marriage or a stronger family? Do you have addictions or distractions that thwart your plans or intentions? Take this quick test to see if your intellectual, emotional, or creative abilities have been stunted in ways you may not have realized.

TEST FOR SELF-RESTRICTION OF INTELLECTUAL, EMOTIONAL, OR CREATIVE GENIUS

Answer "yes" or "no" to the following questions:

1. Do you feel stuck in your life and likely to be passed over for opportunities for joy?

2. Do you often feel that you do not have the abilities to succeed in your goals or dreams?

3. Do you feel that your background has limited your future?

4. Do you often think that you could have advanced farther than

you have but were blocked because of your abilities or circumstances?

5. Do you often fantasize about what "might have happened" in your life, but never pursued the fantasy because it seemed unrealistic?

6. Do you regret the choices you made in your life because you lacked confidence in yourself or felt that you were "over your head" in expectations versus abilities?

7. Are you unhappy with your relationship or marriage because it has hit a barrier of intimacy and depth?

8. Are you unhappy or dissatisfied with your job and your progress toward a better or more exciting work life?

9. Are you unhappy with your life as it is, compared with where you want to be?

10. Do you feel totally unprepared to meet a major challenge to your life's goals or to survive the unexpected possibility of your worst nightmare?

If you answered "yes" to one of these questions, then you are probably passing through a negative cycle in your life. If you answered "yes" to two or more, it is highly likely that you have suffered a trauma to your neurological network and your psychological potential. You will find helpful and even life-changing information in the pages that follow. Joy, peace, and fulfillment can be yours, so why settle for anything else?

NO BULL

Before we get any farther down the road, let me assure you that this is not inspirational bull that I'm tossing around for my own benefit. I'm not pitching attitude therapy, psychotherapy, pills, or religion. I do not believe in "positive thinking" as the definitive answer to anyone's problems. In my experience, the concept of positive thinking is just another way of saying that you are trying to overlay your basic pessimistic thoughts with a coating of crapola. There may be short-term benefits to telling yourself over and over "I can change my life," or "I can make a million dollars," but as far as I can tell there are no lasting positive effects.

Twelve Facts of IQ (*Psychology Today*, July/August 2001)

1. IQ correlates with simple abilities

2. IQ is affected by school attendance

3. IQ is not affected by birth order

4. IQ is related to breast-feeding

5. IQ varies by birth date

6. IQ evens out with age

7. Intelligence is plural, not singular (multiple abilities)

8. IQ is correlated with head size

9. Intelligence scores are predictive of real-world outcomes

10. Intelligence is cortex-specific

11. IQ is on the rise

12. IQ is influenced by the school cafeteria menu

You do need to understand that, although your life may have come to a dead end, you have survived. And the reason you have survived is that you still have some skills that can be built upon. You may have failed the test but it wasn't because you are stupid. You failed because you did not know *how to pass*. We're going to get to the "how" very quickly. When people come to me for vocational counseling, I often hear, "I am no good at being a _____ [teacher, mechanic, etc.]. I need to go back and start over again."

Not so fast, I tell them. And I'm telling you the same thing now. What you have learned so far has value. So don't throw it out. Build on it. Assume you wanted to trade in your old car for a newer one because you were feeling that it would soon be beyond its usefulness and prestige, but the salesman informed you that your old car was far more worthwhile than the newer one. Maybe it has become a collector's item. Would you go ahead and buy the newer car because you are addicted to having new things, or would you enjoy your collector's car? Your answer may tell you the truth about your inner feelings. The choice of a new car might imply disregard for the riches of true value.

Here's the concept: You don't have to toss out the old you just because you have not realized your full potential. But you can learn new skills to fully realize your gifts. You are unique and of great value to the world, so let's not worry about trying to be somebody else. Let's help you unleash all of the creativity, love, joy, and intellect that you are capable of presenting to the universe. I'm going to give you step-by-step processes backed by the best science available to help you accomplish this. The results will come quickly, and they will change your life.

THE BASICS: QUANTUM PHYSICS AND NEUROLOGICAL PLASTICITY

A major statement I want to make is that I am a career human scientist and I don't just say what you may want to hear. The information in this book is based on scientific findings and clinical research. This is not purely inspirational material. It *is* inspirational, but there are real underlying studies supporting these remarkable discoveries. There has been some very exciting science in the last two years that substantiates my approach based on physics, neurology, and the behavioral sciences. Let's start with microscience, the study of the atoms of matter, which takes us into quantum physics. The word *quantum* in physics was first applied when Max Planck found that atomic particles appeared to take leaps in their behavior, such as changing color immediately. For example, light would change from blue to green with no gradual shift. This quantum leap cannot be explained by the usual gradients of measurement, such as the temperature of water as it cools or heats up.

Further investigation by such scientists as Albert Einstein revealed that atomic particles would take these quantum leaps in and out of existence often. But what was most astounding was that these tiny sources of energy were under the influence of the scientist's consciousness. As Werner Heisenberg would later demonstrate, the location of a particle depended on where the investigator looked. The purpose of this physics stuff is to illustrate that you can change your physical makeup by reshuffling your brain connections in the same way you can change your mind. Cool, huh? Intentions (i.e., consciousness) can play a role in constructing the world as we see and experience it. You can actually get physically stronger by engaging in the mental exercises I will show you.

Here's another example: In computer science we use the term *bit,* which is a measure of information. A "bit" of information relates to one piece of data. For example, the datum "$5.00" is a single bit of information. The brain is capable of processing 1,000,000,000,000 times 1,000,000,000,000 bits of information per second, and an average high-speed computer has a capacity of about 33,000,000 bits per second. For any given day, you are presented with at least a million bits of information—the temperature, the traffic, your family demands, etc. The average human being processes only 2,000 of these bits a day.

If we are processing only a small fraction of our capability, then we are limiting our potential. Why do we have such a narrow focus? Let's look more deeply into the actual function of our brains. We will see that the brain too responds to what we imagine to be true, instead of giving us a totally objective view of the real world. The brain does not see or hear events directly. It goes through a two-step process.

The first step includes our sensory channels, such as visual (sight), auditory (hearing), tactile (touch), olfactory (smell), and kinesthetic (balance). These senses feed vibrational energies into the brain. Light rays, for example, stimulate the retina of the eyes and nerve impulses are sent to the brain. The second step happens as the sensory impulses are sent to the brain for interpretation. There they are connected with a series of memory and knowledge nerves that try to identify the impulses based on stored information. This explains why we can "see" only what we know. Unless we have knowledge or memory of some sensation, our brains do not recognize it. I have demonstrated to patients many times that although they may have been measured to have average mental abilities, I can help them perform or "see" at very high levels of cognitive functioning. But because this information is so rare to them, they cannot remember it the next day.

I also observed this when I watched a group of people learn how to walk on hot coals during a training exercise. Yet when I showed photographs of the exercise to several of the same coal-walkers the next day, they refused to believe they'd done it. Sports history is full of examples of athletes who perform above and beyond all expectations at some point in their lives. My favorite is Bob Beamon, the world record holder for the long jump. At the Mexico City Olympics in 1968, Beamon was little known. Few people, including Beamon, had any great expectations for him. Yet before his jump, he felt a strange calm and a sense of unlimited possibility. As he began to run toward the pit, something was triggered in his consciousness. He soared two feet farther than any human being had ever leaped, an extraordinary achievement. Yet he was not aware of his feat until he moved toward the center of the field to don his warmups. When he was told what he had done, he became so disoriented that he got sick to his stomach. Interestingly, he was never able to match that mark, or even to come close to it.

Realize that there are no limits to your performance either. Each of us is capable of defying all expectations, even our own. You may feel stuck, in a rut, or at a dead end, but that is simply a feeling. It does not have to be your reality. The only limits you have are those that you place on yourself. This neurological and psychological principle of self-denial will be the hardest challenge for you. Too often, we take comfort in our limitations. We live down to low expectations. We hide in the comfort zone and wallow in our insecurities. Even those who are certifiably smart suffer from this. It's said that the most frequent dream of professors is that their ignorance will be discovered and their Ph.D.s will be snatched away.

Our minds really do play tricks on us, but sometimes we play tricks on our minds too. The authority on this is Candace Pert, my personal nominee for a Nobel Prize. She has done great work on the nature of neurotransmitters by unlocking the mystery of neuroplasticity. Neuroplasticity is the ability of the brain to continually remold its function based on its needs and new possibilities. Unfortunately, it can serve destructive needs as well as constructive. In a nutshell, this is how it works. There are billions of nerve connections that make up the brain. The junctions between these nerves are called *synapses*. These synapses act like the plugs in the electrical outlets of our homes. The wall outlets in our nervous system are called *receptor sites*. The good news is that we can grow new receptor sites and change their locations based on the constant changes in our brains. As we continue to focus on our perceived realities and our challenges, these synapses begin to change and even multiply around some major transmissions.

Dr. Pert has brilliantly shown us how these changes are modified through our emotional associations. She has also demonstrated how these combinations affect our immune functions and other physiological aspects of our existence. Emotional associations can suffocate our brains. If mathematics baffles you, it is likely that you'll go into a big math test with fears that could trigger depression and anxiety. This may signal your brain to go into protective mode whenever you are faced with a math test. You become hardwired to shut down at the sight of an algebra quiz. The brain's neurotransmitters transform your perceived math phobia into a reality. The good or bad news is that as these nerve cells die and are reborn, they replicate and multiply the effects of previous events, so we either grow smarter or even more muddled by math.

Science continues to open new frontiers to all of us. No longer are we restricted to the genetic brain capacities we inherited from our parents. Based on a recent review of over two hundred studies published in *Nature,* Bernard Devlin concluded that at least 52 percent (certainly more than half) of the brain's function is based on our prenatal care, education, and how we stimulate our brains. The brain does reach its optimal stages around the age of twenty-six, but it continues to develop for the rest of our lives.

According to the national assessment conducted every ten years and funded by the National Institute of Mental Health in 2002, a survey of 9,282 people revealed that one in four people develops at least one mental disorder in a given year. One in seventeen develops a condition severe enough to warrant professional treatment. Three-quarters of people who developed anxiety, impulse control, and substance abuse problems did so by age twenty-one. Anxiety disorders (social phobias and panic disorders) had been experienced by 29 percent. Impulse disorders, including attention-deficit disorder, were 25 percent and 9 percent respectively.

So you can always improve your brainpower. There is no reason to accept limitations or restrictions from within or from others. The phrase "Use it or lose it" applies to your brain. We need to push our mental capacities or risk having the brain kick into sleep or safe mode from lack of stimulation. If you see your life as drab and unchanging, imagine how your brain must feel! I don't want you to worry that your brain is rotting—anxiety will only make things worse. Instead, I am going to show you how to stimulate your mind and get your life on a creative, positive, and fulfilling track. This is the opportunity to discover who you really are and to catch a glimpse of the magical possibilities that await you.

MAKE A DECISION TO REAWAKEN YOUR DREAMS AND PASSIONS

The first step is to realize that you have no real limitations. Then, you need to open your mind to the possibilities that exist for you. Your first step will be challenging, but stimulating too. You can open the doors to literally anything and everything you want in life. You can't compare what lies ahead to what has occurred in the past. You have to adopt a whole new frame of reference. The power lies within you, and I can give you the tools to become the person you were meant to be—you simply have to believe in the possibilities.

There is no reason for you to accept "average" grades or levels of performance. Nobody was born to be mediocre, so don't accept mediocrity in any aspect of your life. We can each find a way to overcome whatever has held us back or slowed us down. Insecurities, depression, anxiety, ADD, and even brain trauma are all challenges that can be overcome. These conditions not only can be overcome, they can even be used to work in your favor. Creative individuals and entrepreneurs can find enormous resources in those academic areas in which they were once not particularly strong and make new discoveries that can enhance their current pursuits. There are preventive measures to help you greatly reduce risk from a stroke, Alzheimer's, or Parkinson's. The truth is that there are excellent avenues to overcoming every one of these traps by learning how to free the "genius within."

The mind is part of the nerve complex we call the brain, but it is also much more. I am the supervising psychologist for American Mensa, also known as "The High IQ Society." I measure intellectual levels for people on a regular basis. I am an expert on the human intellect and true intelligence. Some people have high IQs as determined by intellectual tests, but that is only one measure of true intelligence. "Street smarts" are every bit as real and may be even more useful. Artistic genius also exists. In fact, genius is the intelligence that resides within each of us. Your intellect is more than material you memorized in school. Your grade point average and the diploma on the wall are only small measures of your true intellectual capacities.

UNLIKELY INTELLIGENCE: COULD YOU BE AMONG THIS GROUP?

There are many "unlikely" millionaires, multimillionaires, billionaires, and great leaders in the world. Bill Gates, Thomas Edison, and Albert Einstein were all judged to have low prospects at one time or another in their lives. Do you ever wonder how some people become superstars in their fields even though they supposedly had little talent or average skills? Michael Jordan cuts an imposing figure, but so do 99 percent of those who play professional basketball. So why did the young man who was cut from his high school's junior varsity team soar above all of the others during his career? Time and again, his competitors talk about his mental toughness, his determination, and his deep understanding of the game.

Your body has physical limitations. But your mind can soar above and beyond what you think is possible. There may be challenges to your mental performance, like an accident that causes trauma to the brain or a mental disorder that slows brain function, but the brain is a remarkable organ. It can be stimulated to heal itself. It can create new pathways for enhanced learning and creative breakthroughs. It is an incredible resource. Know that, and accept no limitations. Anything is possible for you! Let's begin your mind-expanding journey to new levels of accomplishment and fulfillment!

Two

THE BREATHING BRAIN

Brian was a very frustrated young man. He barely passed seventh and eighth grades even though he had scored high on standardized tests. By the first three weeks of his freshman year in high school he was lost. His parents let him know that he was not meeting their high expectations.

Brian wanted his family to be proud of him. He dreamed of going on to medical school one day. But with his mounting failures, he felt he might have set his goals too high. Depression set in, eroding his friendships and further hampering his performance in the classroom. A concerned school counselor referred Brian to my clinic to be evaluated for attention deficit disorder (ADD) because of his difficulty focusing on class work.

My evaluation found that Brian did not have the typical brain function pattern of a person with ADD, but he definitely did have problems focusing his attention. I noticed that when Brian attempted challenging memory tasks, his anxiety levels rose significantly. Stress levels that high would impact his work in school, without a doubt. But I noticed a more telling sign that clued me in to the root causes of Brian's problems in school. As his anxiety increased he would begin to hyperventilate, which robbed him of the ability to focus. It was more of a neurological block than I had anticipated.

The most efficient breath rate is twelve to fourteen breaths a minute. When he wasn't hyperventilating, Brian was breathing at a rate of five breaths per minute. It was scary, almost as if he wasn't breathing at all. We could hardly detect any rise or fall of his chest. It was a wonder that

According to David C. Page, author of *Your Jaws—Your Life,* it is better to breathe through your nose because it stimulates the release of nitric oxide, which enhances mental activity, especially creativity. In fact, there is a high correlation between mouth breathing and heart attacks. Mouth breathing, especially during the night (snoring), can deprive the brain of oxygen and cause cardiovascular problems. Mouth breathing is also correlated with attention deficit disorder.

he could even walk with so little breathing activity. Brian was close to being a real-life zombie, though I didn't feel I should share that particular diagnosis with him.

Interestingly, this was a zombie who ran track. Brian was on the team, but he wasn't exactly running at an Olympic pace. More like a glacial pace. He was a motivated, aggressive young man with a solid physique, yet he ran like he was carrying a baby grand piano on his back. This fit kid was the slowest on the team, for no apparent reason. I questioned Brian about his mental approach to running. I had noticed that he ran with a tense, grim look on his face. He reminded me of those ancient Greek military runners who were always being sent off from the battle-fields to deliver bad news to the cruel king. Brian explained that he'd seen faster athletes, his role models, run with their faces set in that tense expression. For some reason, he assumed they looked like that because they were holding their breath as they ran. Brian didn't draw in air as he ran sprints in practice, which, as you might expect, severely limited the distance he could cover without pooping out (to use a scientific term).

Even worse, Brian had developed the habit of not breathing whenever he felt stressed, as when doing schoolwork like math problems or history essays. I was once a high school coach so I'd been around the track a few times. I made a suggestion to Brian's track coach, Tommy Hinson, that we put Brian on the cross-country running team. Brian was not impressed with the revival of my coaching career. "I can't run a hundred yards without falling over and you want me to run ten miles?"

I told him that he might surprise himself, but that he could stop and walk anytime he wanted in the early phases of his training. "Just finish the practice course before the sun goes down so we can find your body," his coach teased.

During the first practice run of five miles, Brian walked a lot, but interestingly enough, he did not come in last. During the second practice run, he did not slow down to walk. He figured out that he could keep going if he maintained a steady, comfortable pace. Brian was finishing among the top three runners on the team by his second week of practice. His confidence was growing to the point that he actually looked forward to the workouts. He moved up quickly in the team rankings and by the next fall, he was leading the pack in meets with other teams. Since we're in the happy-ending business, you'd be right to suspect that Brian's performance in the classroom also improved dramatically once he learned to keep the air flowing to his body and brain. He became a leading math student, and was accepted in the Honor Society his junior year. He eventually earned a Ph.D. in economics, became a successful musician, and founded a great business. Luckily, he remembered "the little people" in his life and we remained friends. I asked him recently what made the difference in his life and he said, "You taught me to breathe for success."

Aha! If only life was so simple, right? Well, sometimes complex solutions begin with simple steps. The great strides Brian made in his life began with adjustments to his breathing patterns and triggered new approaches and attitudes. The improvements in his breathing pattern would not have done it alone. But it was a first step toward adjusting his brain patterns and changing the way he approached challenges. Remember, if you haven't been getting the results you want with the patterns you've been following in your life, you have to change those patterns.

WHY DOES CHANGING YOUR BREATHING MAKE A DIFFERENCE?

We need air to live. We also need air to think and function efficiently. Virtually every cell in our bodies requires oxygen, which is most commonly produced through the red blood cells. More than two thousand organ functions are influenced by the levels of oxygen and carbon dioxide in the body, from the health of our skin to the rhythm of our hearts. The brain is especially sensitive to breathing.

Assessment: Are You an Effective Breather?

You've got to have a plan. But there is no plan without goals, smaller steps toward those goals, and ways to measure your progress. So your plan for adjusting your breathing skills must contain all of those elements, and oxygen, of course.

Answer each of the following statements according to how consistently they apply to your behavior with a rating of Very Consistent, Often Consistent, 50 Percent of the Time Consistent, Rarely Consistent, or Never.

1. In times of stress, such as taking a hard test, I hold my breath as if I am pushing the answers to my brain.

2. When I can't remember something I know I should know, I get frustrated and strain my brain to remember.

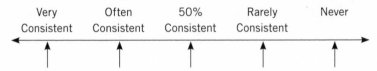

3. My eyes often get tired when I am stressed or have to read a long time.

4. My shoulder and jaw muscles get tight and sore because I get so stressed when I am under pressure.

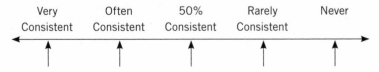

5. My vision gets blurry when I am under stress.

6. I start yawning or hiccupping when I take tests.

7. I get stomach butterflies, stomachaches, or even vomit when I get stressed by a test or performance.

8. I have trouble stopping my thinking about one topic or subject in order to shift to another problem.

9. I can't be creative when I am under pressure. I just can't think beyond the usual bad solutions.

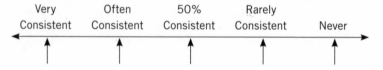

10. I make a lot of simple errors under stress.

11. I can't concentrate and focus on test questions under stress.

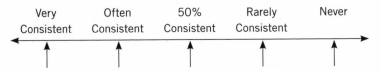

12. I begin to think of a hundred different things rather than the questions and answers.

13. Sometimes I can't take the test seriously, and begin to think only of humorous and cynical responses to the questions.

14. The longer the test is, the more nervous I get.

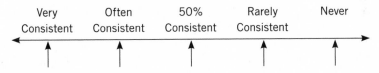

15. I spend a lot of time worrying about the outcome of a test, rather than focusing on what I should do to prepare for it.

Scoring:

If you scored "50 percent" or "often consistent" on any of the items above, learning breathing skills will likely benefit your mental performance. If you scored "very consistent" on any of the items, it is important that you learn good breathing skills, or you may not succeed at the level at which you are capable.

THE WORKS

Next, I want to discuss how breathing patterns affect some very important functions, especially as they relate to performance and stress. What follows is a general map of the brain from the top view showing the basic functions of the outer layer (cortex). You will note that there are some areas that have specific functions associated with them, such as memory in the temporal lobe and organizational abilities in the frontal lobe.

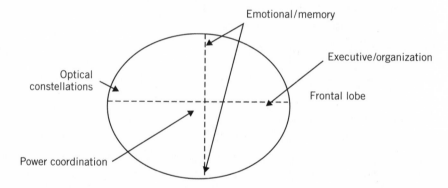

When you take more than fourteen breaths per minute, you signal the rest of your body, especially the brain, that you are stressing out. This triggers the old fight-or-flight response, which has kept humankind in the game since caveman days. This is why your ancestors did not end up as lunch at the Saber-toothed Tiger Cafeteria.

Try this experiment: Purposely breathe at a rate of twenty cycles per minute. After two minutes of this, if someone hasn't called the guys in white coats, you'll note that you feel agitated. That's because you've triggered some very primal instincts. Rapid breathing stimulates emotional and physical responses that are hardwired into the brain. If you begin to hyperventilate (very high respiration cycles), you trigger a panic pattern in your mind. The natural response when you are in panic is to seek a cause. Sometimes, we attribute the panic to the wrong cause and that gives us a phobia, also known as an irrational fear. Some people have very low respiration rates. Sometimes mistaken for the "living dead," they slink around with sunken chests and their chins tucked into their necks. I wonder how they retain consciousness with such low oxygen intake. These people always seem to be in line ahead of me at the airport. Either that, or they are running security for my line at the airport.

Try this experiment: Slump over and breathe as slowly as you can. After three minutes, you may begin to feel depressed. You lose energy and become somber, which is only natural because if you continued this breathing pattern for very long you'd be likely headed to a funeral soon: your own.

I have "cured" many depressed or panicky patients in one session simply by teaching them to breathe correctly. Sometimes, my friends, it is possible even for humans to "win by a nose."

FIVE BREATHING STRATEGIES

I have studied breathing techniques for many years because proper breathing is the most direct route for teaching the brain what you want it to do. I have found it especially useful in times of crisis as it facilitates the body's own natural healing processes. I led a team of experts on a research project in which we taught breathing techniques to a group of patients undergoing spinal surgery. We compared them with a group of patients undergoing the same surgery without the training. The results were very revealing. Our trained breathing group had no complications, healed twice as fast, and had significantly lower pain levels than the comparison group.

Breathing is as easy as, well, breathing, once you do it in the proper way. It's the epitome of natural healing. Here are techniques for learning to control your breathing patterns to improve your health and performance.

1. Diaphragmatic

The most practiced of breathing techniques and the one I used for the surgery study is called the diaphragmatic pattern. This approach focuses on using the diaphragm, which is located at the bottom of the lungs. You might consider using this breathing pattern if you need to learn new material or call up an image, such as visualizing how a word is spelled or to remember someone's name. It is also a very powerful tool for mobilizing your strengths. Many people deal with challenges such as physical pain by using imagery and tapping into the body's natural healing powers. The diaphragmatic pattern can be learned by putting your hand on your belly button. Breathe in and out and note how your hand moves up and down. That's your diaphragm at work, bringing air into your lungs.

When treating a youngster, I'll paint a big circle on the child's hand and place it over his or her stomach. Then I'll tell the child to breathe into the circle. When done correctly, the child begins to breathe at a rate of twelve to fourteen cycles per minute. It also works to have the patient breathe in for seven counts and out for seven counts.

I know. This breathing method is boring. So let your mind wander. Just keep counting and breathing. One warning, it may put you to sleep. But that's relaxing too, isn't it?

Brain scans show that areas of memory light up when proper breathing techniques are used. This is an indication that good breathing helps trigger creativity. Let me recommend an experiment. Do a pre-test of memory by having a friend read you the following telephone numbers (fictitious), along with the names associated with these numbers. After hearing each number and name, see if you can remember each person's number. (A perfect score would be all three numbers remembered and recounted.)

- Tom   214-559-2665

- Mary   505-456-8282

- Ray   912-554-2334

Now spend at least five minutes using the diaphragmatic breathing technique; repeat the procedure and compare your response. You can use this method to prepare for a test in the same way.

Here is a real-life example of how powerful this breathing technique can be. Sean, the son of a lawyer, had completed law school but was having difficulty passing the bar exam. He would make careless mistakes, such as missing a whole page of questions. His psychotherapist suggested that Sean was unconsciously trying to fail because he did not want to be compared to his father, a very successful lawyer. I taught him a controlled breathing technique and he passed the bar with the highest score in his group. Still, Sean never did practice law. Instead, he went into business as a forensic consultant and had great success. So maybe his psychotherapist had a point, too.

2. Full Breath

This similar technique uses all breathing levels—the chest, the stomach, and the shoulders—not just the diaphragmatic level. This pattern can be helpful when you are very anxious and need to gain some emotional control. You may be angry or stressed. By breathing in this pattern you regain your sense of composure. This is also an extremely helpful pattern for controlling anxiety when you are trying to make big decisions.

I usually teach this method with one hand on the patient's navel and the other on the patient's chest. I have the patient begin to breathe at my lower hand while keeping the chest stable. Then, after sixty seconds, I have the patient breathe so that only the chest area is moving and the stomach area remains stable. This can be very tricky for some individuals and they may need some coaching.

After sixty seconds, I advise the patient to try to breathe only through the shoulders by slightly raising them up with each inhalation while keeping both the chest and stomach stable. After thirty seconds, I'll tell the patient to begin to breathe by moving all three areas (chest, stomach, and shoulders). It takes a little practice, but most people report a sense of relaxation very quickly as they open up their capacities to breathe more efficiently.

This method is fun to watch on the brain monitor because it shows a beautiful blend of frequencies. It's like a symphony in which all the instruments blend together in perfect harmony. And, staying with that metaphor, this method helps people get into harmony with themselves. When you experience stress and tension, it is often because you are not centered or emotionally stable. Little things bother you and knock you off balance. When you feel out of synch and edgy, use this technique to get back on track.

Think of a very stressful situation in your life, such as having a spat with a spouse or giving a speech to a big group. Rate how stressful this situation is to you with a ranking from 1 (low impact) to 10 (highest impact). While you are imagining this situation, assume the full breath pattern for five minutes, and if you are still thinking of your problem and haven't dismissed it, rate how stressful it is to you now using the same 1–10 scale. This can be a very important method of letting go of stress and burdens when you need to be strong to meet a challenge.

3. The Triangle (1-4-2)

This breathing pattern is the most popular, especially with people who have trouble sleeping. Jean, like half of the people in this country, had difficulty sleeping. She'd be lucky to get in three hours of true rest a night. She was also seriously overweight so she was battling that problem as well. Weight gain often accompanies a lack of restorative sleep— it's a double penalty. (Nobody said life was fair.) But with my help, Jean learned techniques for creating a restful pattern of sleep. Once she'd mastered the technique, she began to lose weight and even participated in a weight-loss challenge on the television show of a certain psychologist friend of mine. (I'm trying not to drop names here.)

The triangle breathing pattern is designed for triggering creativity and inspiration. If you've been racking your brain for a new approach to a problem at work, this technique may help you find that "outside the box" solution. The triangle breathing pattern is based on a ratio of 1:4:2. For every one count of breathing in, hold that breath for four counts, and exhale for two counts. That pattern is usually too rapid for most of us, so the typical count is 4:16:8, which entails breathing in to a count of four (1-2-3-4 inhalation) holding that breath for sixteen counts (1-2-3-4-5-6-7-8-9-10-11-12-13-14-15-16), and exhaling it slowly to a count of eight (1-2-3-4-5-6-7-8). Sounds complicated, I know. Some people need a CD, cassette, or metronome to help them stay on track. If you can do it for ten minutes, it can be effective in focusing your mind.

When this method was tested, the brain monitor showed the back of the brain lighting up. That's where the power of imagery is based. There was also heightened activity in the frontal lobes where organizational abilities are centered. Albert Einstein and Thomas Edison were both said to use this technique. Edison would hang his head over a plate of water with pebbles in his hands. He would concentrate on challenges and allow his brain to enter a sleepy, drowsy state. When he was about to go to sleep, his hands would loosen their grip on the pebbles and the water would splash on his face, which kept him alert enough to maintain the free-association state.

To see if this is relevant to your challenges, think of a really difficult but specific question that you have to find the answer to. Breathe with the triangle technique for ten minutes, holding the question or challenge in your mind. Try to remember everything that comes to you in detail. As soon as the session is over, record your experience in some way. Write it down, make a video, tell a friend, or just tape-record your recollection. Then, reflect on the experience and see if the difficult answer presents itself. It's almost like magic, isn't it? That's the power of tapping into your mind in a relaxed state.

4. Alternate Nostrils

It's okay to have fun with this one but as strange as it sounds, it is rooted in ancient East Indian practices. It is a method for breaking thought patterns when you are stuck or can't seem to escape self-defeating behaviors. Maybe you can't stop thinking about someone who hurt your feelings. Or maybe you have been obsessing over an upcoming test or job interview. This is a way to break free of that pattern so you can focus your mind on more constructive thinking.

The method is to consciously breathe through alternate nostrils. Don't worry—unless you have muscles in places where most people have only cartilage, it's okay to press your fingers to the outside of your nostrils to accomplish this process. Breathe in one nostril by closing off the other, and when you've inhaled all you can, close that nostril and breathe out through the other. (It might be wise not to do this where narcotics officers are hanging out.) Then, maintaining that same side, breathe in and release on the other nostril. Repeat the alternating pattern several times in a relaxed manner. If you were viewing your brain on a brain monitor, you'd notice something very interesting happening. The image of your brain lights up, one section after the other. First, it might be your temporal lobes, then your frontal lobe, then toward the back, or in some other progression. It is like watching a neon message board flickering on at various times. It may seem chaotic, but out of chaos comes calm. Your brain is doing a reshuffle. It is clearing connections so that you can find a fresh solution.

You can experiment with this technique by focusing on a problem or concern that has been nagging you like a song playing over and over in your mind. Remember that your goal is to get unstuck from the nagging thought or problem. You will feel some confusion after two or three minutes and you might want to stop, but don't. Keep breathing in this pattern until you can no longer think about the problem. You are cleansing your mind.

This technique worked well for Tom, who had a lot of worries. He'd been diagnosed with lung cancer and, not surprisingly, he'd become obsessed with dying from it. That was all he could think about, every waking hour—and since he couldn't sleep, that meant twenty-four hours a day. It was understandable, of course, but his concern about dying was becoming more debilitating than the cancer itself.

I helped Tom master the alternate nostril breathing technique and it enabled him to conquer his fear. He realized that he didn't have to be a victim of cancer, he could be a fighter instead. He shifted his thinking so he could cope with the challenge and he eventually became a cancer survivor who helped others deal with similar challenges.

5. Box Breathing (4-4-4-4)

Box breathing is often used for dealing with fear. This technique is based on a "square" formula of 4-4-4-4 counts, meaning you breathe in for a count of four (1-2-3-4), hold it for a count of four (1-2-3-4), exhale to the count of four (1-2-3-4), and do not breathe in for a count of four (1-2-3-4). The final step is the clincher. Fears tend to surface rapidly when you can't breathe.

Your brain, wondrous mechanism that it is, associates your fear with the lack of air. As you begin to panic just a bit, the fears you've been harboring come to the surface. But if you follow through with the process, you will get beyond the panic and your brain will wash away the fear. Jim, a jazz pianist, had become all but paralyzed by a fear of making mistakes in front of an audience. He would become violently sick to his stomach before a performance because of his fear. I suggested we try the box breathing, and after forty-five seconds, Jim started getting anxious. He said he was afraid he might pass out.

I reassured him and he continued, but he struggled each time with the last breath. It took some comforting, but I got him to continue the pattern in spite of his misgivings. After five minutes he began to relax and, wonder of wonders, he even smiled. I saw a new look of determination in his eyes. As he relaxed, he became more confident in his playing. He also learned to enjoy performing in front of a big audience.

If you are having trouble with a nagging thought or concern, try one of these breathing techniques for at least ten minutes. Don't be surprised if you forget one set of fears and suddenly begin to focus on even larger ones—this is normal and just a step in the process. If you stick with it, you'll confront your anxieties and make a breakthrough!

SOME FINAL THOUGHTS

Breathing techniques have been used to assert control for hundreds of years. They can be very powerful tools, yet we often dismiss them too easily. They are time-proven methods for controlling anxiety and unreasonable fears—and they're also much cheaper than prescription drugs.

Remember that you will get better with practice. I would suggest you employ these breathing techniques once a day or in combination with another activity.

Three

BRAIN DETOXIFICATION

Like most fourteen-year-olds, Katie struggled with self-esteem and felt awkward. Still, she had been an honor student in her elementary school and she was looking forward to the challenges of high school. But once she got there, poor Katie crashed and burned. Her grades plummeted and she became a social recluse, abandoning all of her friends. Her parents were shocked when she was placed in special education classes. They brought her to the Lawlis and Peavey Center for tests to determine if she had attention deficit disorder or some form of schizophrenia.

Katie's problems were not simple. We found that her brain was not getting the nutrients it needed because of two factors. She had a yeast-type growth in her intestines that prevented food from being metabolized correctly. She also had a poor diet, which can cause a lot of problems for an adolescent going through puberty. The quality of her schoolwork declined because Katie's brain was too hungry to think. Her memory went blank, and the part of her brain that normally handled organizational skills went on strike. She was suffering from neurological malnutrition that kept her from accomplishing her schoolwork. It resulted in memory failure and problems getting organized, and those brain blips, in turn, resulted in lowered self-esteem. She didn't feel good about herself so she didn't feel comfortable around other people. Katie had the typical teen trauma—times ten. And it was all because she wasn't giving her brain the fuel it needed to function.

She also had some family issues. Katie had two brothers who treated her like one of the guys until she started developing. All of a sudden, little sister became a woman. She was suddenly a stranger to them. A sexy stranger. They stopped treating her like their sister and, quite naturally, it threw her off. In addition, her transition into womanhood caused her father to pull back emotionally. He didn't know how to relate to his daughter once she'd matured. It's not unusual for fathers of girls to have difficulty making this adjustment.

Dr. Karin Michaels of Brigham and Women's Hospital in Boston reported in the *International Journal of Cancer* that young girls who ate french fries at ages three to five increased their chances of getting breast cancer by 27 percent.

With all that she had going on emotionally, and the little fuel that she had going in physically, it was no wonder that Katie hit a wall. Teenage brains rewire. Hers short-circuited. We conducted a brain scan and found that her whole brain had shut down from malnourishment. It was also in a diminished stage known as "diffusion," in which messages don't move through the brain at the usual rate.

The good news is that Katie's problems, as complex as they were, proved to be highly treatable. Her fungal infection was eliminated within a month or two, thanks to proper medication. Regular, balanced meals put her brain back in high gear and her grades improved dramatically, enabling her to return to mainstream classes. And her social life also made a comeback as her self-esteem climbed and it dawned on her peers that Katie was not only smart, she was pretty darned cute.

We also did some counseling with her family. Her father learned it was okay to treat her the way he always had, and her brothers adjusted their attitudes and quit ganging up on her just because they didn't know how else to respond to this new girl/woman in their midst.

The teenage years are loaded with neurological challenges as teenage brains rewire themselves. That explains why teens "space out"—it's not that they are space cadets or dopes, it's because their brains sporadically shut down for rewiring just as your office computer system shuts down for repairs and updates from time to time. One of my friends used humor—and pretty good science—when her teens hit this stage. Instead of yelling at them or punishing them, she would order them to "Engage frontal lobes!" You see, during adolescence the brain specializes. It shuts down in some areas and rewires in others, making new connections. This process causes some loss in frontal lobe connections and associated areas where judgment and planning are centered. It explains why teenagers seem to lack "common sense." And it is also why they don't think or plan for the long term.

Studies published in July 2005 in the *Archives of Pediatrics and Adolescent Medicine* concluded that television viewing tended to have an adverse effect on children's academic pursuits. Children in the third grade (approximately eight years old) who had televisions in their bedrooms (and watched more television) scored lower on standardized tests than those those who did not have sets in their rooms. The American Academy of Pediatrics has urged parents to limit children's television viewing to no more than one to two hours per day.

Katie's adolescent brain blip might have created, briefly, a teenage zombie. But like most teens, she survived and, ultimately, thrived. She went through once-in-a-lifetime changes and she emerged stronger and more resilient, with a little help and understanding.

Katie got the help she needed. Other teens turn to drugs or worse to get them through these incredibly challenging years. What they don't realize is that marijuana and other drugs interfere with their neurochemistry at a time when the teen brain can't handle additional challenges. The impact can last a lifetime.

TOXICITY OF THE BRAIN

The brain is a very highly evolved and complex mechanism that we barely understand even with our highly evolved and complex brains. When it doesn't function well, the problem is most likely somewhere south of the forehead—in other words, it's not the brain's fault. Brains are the most reactive organ in our bodies. It's the organizational center, or control room, for most functions of the body, but the brain also depends on the rest of the body to nurture and protect it.

According to federal government findings, 24 percent of American homes today still contain dangerous levels of lead. This amounts to 24 million homes.

Unfortunately, many doctors and other health care providers don't get it. They don't look at your entire system when considering brain malfunctions. They don't consider that the source of the problem may not be in the control room itself. It could be down in the plumbing, or the fuel pump. It is a fact that 90 percent of the body's source of serotonin, the neurotransmitter that helps control depression and anxiety, resides in the stomach. In many arenas of medicine, the gut is seen as the second brain because the dynamics there are so sensitive to a person's mental stability and cognitive functions. It is true that we often live by our "gut reactions." Katie's case illustrates that some neurological problems are the result of internal biological turmoil. Similarly, problems within the brain can also trigger allergies, so sneezing and itching can be symptomatic of breakdowns in the brain, just as toxic reactions in the brain can be set off by stomachaches, diarrhea, and parasites in the colon. It's a two-way street.

Allergies are the body's reaction to substances that it considers dangers for some reason. A simple dog hair can send some people into meltdowns with runny noses, swollen nasal passages, and labored breathing. Our immune systems have multiple defenses; the most studied are the white blood cells. There are several kinds of white blood cells, but they all function as warriors that destroy our enemies either by eating or by poisoning them, mostly through a combination of both processes. The most numerous of these powerful allies are the neutrophils, which make up about 60 percent of all substances in the bloodstream. These little guys are the front line of defense and are most active when external enemies enter the system. They use poison to kill organisms and swallow them, and then usually die in the process.

The major forces in activating your immunity are histamine and prostaglandins, the indicators of injury and distress in your body. If you have ever had hay fever or been reactive to some substance, you will likely take antihistamine medication to stop the inflammatory reactions. Although the alarm system protects us, it can also harm us. The inflammatory reaction and the poisons that the white blood cells use can cause the destruction of other tissues, and can become overreactive enough to attack your own body. When your immune system begins to overreact, this is called "autoimmune disease" and is responsible for such disorders as arthritis (attacking the joints), lupus (attacking the internal organs), and multiple sclerosis (attacking the nervous system). The immune system can attack the brain because of its direct involvement with the immune system itself, and because it also carries stress messages, whether rational or not, that the immune system perceives as an enemy.

It has been demonstrated in interesting research that there is a definite tendency in children with autism toward "allergy" responses, which dispose them to atypical viral infections and/or candida/yeast infections. In fact, the immune system may play a vital role in producing increased pro-inflammatory cytokines (messenger proteins that activate other immune cell types, such as killer T cells), which would make you more sensitive to dietary proteins.

The fascinating fact is that most of our immune receptors are in our gut, possibly because this is the major entry for a lot of toxins in our body. Once the gut is wounded in any way, it becomes more susceptible to reactions to foods that might ordinarily cause no harm. Pathogenic strains of bacteria and yeast may also promote this immune reaction. This kind of gut problem can also be caused by overuse of antibiotics, which actually strip the gut of important bacteria along with the bad bacteria. In the case of Katie, she had a long history of ear infections, and her use of antibiotics may have been a major player in the overgrowth of yeast, which in turn blocked important enzymes for the nutrition of the brain.

In summary, the brain is greatly influenced by its internal environment. If it is sitting in a sewer of inflammation, it is going to choke and suffer for lack of clean air and nutrients, constantly reacting in alarm. This can be caused by exposure to external agents as well as by our own lifestyles. Like maintaining a fine car, we have the responsibility to get it running in peak condition by providing a clean environment.

Over the past several decades, concerns have been raised over unacceptable levels of environmental toxins. There are between 50,000 and 100,000 synthetic chemicals currently used in commercial production, and new synthetics enter commerce at an average of three per day. How these chemicals affect humans neurologically has not been adequately studied; however, data strongly suggest that we are all vulnerable to neurological damage and autoimmune reactions. Children are especially sensitive to these elements, and because they are smaller and usually closer to the ground than adults, they are therefore more exposed.

IS YOUR BRAIN CONTAMINATED?

The probability is high that your brain has some toxicity interfering with its function, since much of our environment is a toxic stew of pollutants. Before you begin to overreact, it would be helpful to review a symptom checklist. The symptoms below are consistent with various forms of toxicity and immune dysfunction as the result of environmental exposure. Check off those symptoms that apply to you or to a friend or family member who is having some cognitive problems.

TOXICITY PROBLEM CHECKLIST

Symptom	Present?
1. A persistent runny nose, especially indoors	( )
2. Hypersensitive skin or rash (reactive to clothing labels)	( )
3. Itchy or red eyes	( )
4. Sneezing	( )
5. Difficulty in breathing deeply	( )
6. Rapid pulse	( )
7. Increased nervousness	( )
8. Emotional irritability	( )
9. Red ears or cheeks	( )
10. Stomachaches, especially after eating	( )
11. Gas and bloating	( )
12. Constipation or diarrhea	( )
13. Diminished ability to read with concentration	( )
14. Diminished memory	( )
15. Diminished control over emotions	( )
16. Cravings, especially for soy or corn sugar (syrup)	( )

17. Sleep problems   ( )
18. Problems organizing or prioritizing work   ( )
19. Increased aggressiveness   ( )
20. Decreased energy   ( )

If you checked off more than two or three of these symptoms, it may be time to investigate your environment to determine your exposure to any of the substances below. A clue is that newer houses can contain paints or carpets that give off invisible toxic gases. Many people develop sensitivities, resulting in histamine buildup in the brain. New clothes and sheets often have these same problems. On the other hand, old houses often have lead-based paint or lead pipes, which could also produce reactions.

Examine the tables below and the direct impact of substances on cognitive problems as documented in studies. Note that there are overlaps, and these substances may interact with hormone imbalances to create multiple side effects. For example, exposure to lead often interacts with the thyroid gland, and low energy, depression, and low cognitive abilities can result from that one condition alone.

EFFECTS OF EXPOSURE TO HEAVY METALS ON COGNITIVE ABILITIES

Cadmium (common in manufacturing waste)	Motor dysfunction Decreased IQ Hyperactivity Hypoactivity
Lead	Learning difficulties Decreased IQ Impulsivity Attention deficit Hyperactivity Violence
Manganese	Brain damage Motor dysfunction Memory impairment

Attention deficit
Compulsive disorder

Mercury   Visual impairment
                                 Learning disabilities
                                 Attention deficit
                                 Motor dysfunction
                                 Memory impairment

EFFECTS OF EXPOSURE TO SOLVENTS
ON COGNITIVE ABILITIES

Ethanol (alcohol)   Learning difficulties
                                 Attention deficit
                                 Memory impairment
                                 Eating/sleeping disorders
                                 Mental retardation

Styrene   Hypoactivity
                                 Lack of inhibition

Toluene   Learning disabilities
                                 Speech deficits
                                 Motor dysfunction

Trichloroethylene   Hyperactivity
                                 Lack of inhibition

Xylene   Motor dysfunction
                                 Learning difficulties
                                 Memory impairment

EFFECTS OF EXPOSURE TO PESTICIDES
ON COGNITIVE ABILITIES

Organochlorines/DDT   Hyperactivity
                                 Decreased energy/effort
                                 Decreased coordination
                                 Memory impairment

Organophosphates (including DFP, chlorpyrifos, Dursban, diazinon)	Hyperactivity Attention disorders Decreased ability to follow instructions
Pyrethroids (including bioallethrin, deltamethrin, cypermethrin)	Hyperactivity Attention problems

The Environmental Working Group, using data from the USDA and FDA pesticide research bank from 1992 to 1997, has compiled a list of the most contaminated fruits directly available to consumers. It is critical that all fruits and vegetables be washed and even peeled to reduce toxic exposure, as a general practice.

- Apples

- Spinach

- Peaches

- Pears

- Strawberries

- Grapes (especially those from Chile)

- Potatoes

- Red raspberries

- Celery

- Green beans

EFFECTS OF EXPOSURE TO OTHER COMMON SUBSTANCES ON COGNITIVE BEHAVIOR

Nicotine	Hyperactivity Learning disabilities Developmental delays

Dioxins	Learning disabilities
PCBs	Learning disabilities
	Attention deficit
	Hyperactivity
	Memory impairment
Fluoride	Hyperactivity
	Decreased IQ

As you can see, we live in a very caustic environment and our brains receive the worst of it. These harmful elements are in the air we breathe, the water we drink, the food we eat, and the beds we sleep in. Children receive as much as fifteen times the polluted air as adults through school bus exhaust fumes. Exposure increases with high-density populations around

ATTENTIONAL PROBLEMS

Probable Cause	Conceptualization	Ability to Focus	Ability to Shift Attention	Ability to Sustain Attention	Memory
Malnutrition		yes	yes		
Lead exposure				yes	yes
Fetal alcohol		yes		yes	yes
Parasite infections	yes	yes	yes	yes	
Lack of intellectual stimulation			yes		

(From an overview of 30 years of research into attentional problems of children, "A Nosology of Disorders of Attention" by Allan Mirsky and Connie Duncan (NIMH), in *Annals of the New York Academy of Sciences,* 2005)

industries, but the farmer has greater exposure to the products of fertilizers and pesticides. It is hard to hide from these substances, but highly motivated individuals can guard themselves against them through education.

WHAT TO DO ABOUT EXPOSURE: CHELATION?

Rather than make the mistake of diagnosing your own symptoms, I would highly recommend an evaluation with your physician to see if you or your child has been exposed to any one of these elements. But be aware that there are many diagnostic procedures and few of them are reliable. Since most toxic chemicals exist as fat-soluble substances, they are usually hidden, often undetectable in the lymph glands, even in a blood test. Hair tests are often recommended because of their residue in hair cells, but these have proven unreliable from one test to the next.

The tests we use are urine samples evaluated by the Great Smokies Lab after two days of oral chelation. Chelation is a term that generally refers to the binding of a metabolic compound to metallic molecules in order to stabilize them and allow them to be excreted without further interaction with the body, thus cleansing the system of metallic elements. In earlier times there were procedures for the cleansing of the cardiovascular system by chelating the entire blood system, and this therapy still has proponents. There are more recent developments, however, and what we use at the Centers for Psychoneurological Change is an oral chelation agent, DSMA (meso-1, dimercaptosuccinic acid), so that the substances can be expelled through urination.

Regardless of what method is used, you have to know what you are dealing with in order to determine the proper procedure. It may be necessary to test repeatedly to see if progress is being made, since many people continue to be exposed in their homes or jobs. These nasty toxic compounds can cause a lot of human suffering, and since they are so common, follow-up visits and regular checkups may be required.

TREATMENT: STIMULATING THE BODY'S NATURAL CLEANSING ENZYMES

There are many medical professionals more expert than I on the reduction of exposure to toxic substances in the body. Dr. Andrew Messamore at the PNP Center advises using DMSA for two days and off for two weeks with supplemental multiple vitamins and minerals for one cycle. As many as four to ten cycles may be necessary.

Additional substances that aid in the detoxification process are (use the advised dosages on the labels, and of course, *always* consult your physician before beginning any new regimen):

1. Milk thistle—used as a liver protectant.

2. Calcium D-glucarate—a calcium salt of D-glucaric acid. Allows for increased net elimination of toxins and steroid hormones.

3. N-acetyl-L-cysteine (NAC)—produces a dramatic acceleration of urinary methylmercury excretion in animals and reduces liver damage.

4. Alpha-ketoglutarate (AKG)—helps detoxify ammonia, synthesized from urea in the colon, often associated with Rett syndrome in children. Very effective as an antioxidative agent.

5. Methyl sulfonyl methane (MSM)—a naturally occurring sulfur compound used in detoxification processes.

6. Taurine—a conditional essential amino acid that appears to inhibit catecholamine oxidation in the brain. Taurine is also required for the formation of bile salts, an important mode of toxin elimination.

7. Methionine—a sulfur-bearing amino acid found in animal proteins that assists in the removal process of heavy metals as well as aiding in their excretion through the urine.

8. Choline—acting as a neurotransmitter as well as metabolism enhancer, this ingredient is very important at the cellular level of detoxification. Individuals who consume a choline-deficit diet often develop hepatic disease.

9. Betaine anhydrous—also known as trimethylglycine, this is a major metabolite of choline. This substance is usually found in small amounts in beets, spinach, and seafood.

10. Selenium—required for the synthesis of a vital antioxidant enzyme that helps detoxify hydrogen peroxide reproduced within cells.

SUPPLEMENTS FOR NEUROLOGICAL DISORDERS DUE TO TOXICITY

The direct influence of nutrition on both the structure and the function of the human brain is rapidly being identified and elucidated by investigative researchers and clinical communities. Over the past several decades of study and especially over the last ten years, in which brain maps have shown precise images of the working brain, a framework is emerging that provides a scientific basis for nutritional supplements and their critical importance. Most important, much ancient wisdom and clinical intuition is being substantiated, allowing those individuals who suffer diminishment of intellectual power to prosper with special nutrients and botanicals.

The following list contains a small set of supplements that have been documented as benefiting individuals with neurological problems related to toxicity and therefore might be considered healing substances. They certainly appear to have a powerful impact, although it is strongly suggested that you get instructions and information from a medical professional in order to have the safest and most immediate impact. (Use the published dosages on the labels as guides.)

1. Acetyl-carnitine has been used for improvement of several neurological problems, including memory, concentration, and mood. This substance occurs naturally in the body as an enhancer of cellular energy by acting as a shuttle between the cytoplasm and the mitochondria for fatty acids. It may also increase choline activity, facilitating serotonin pathways, and enhance synaptic transmission.

2. Coenzyme Q10 (also known as CoQ10 or ubiquinone) has been used for mood and memory enhancement. It has been documented that it provides antioxidant benefits as well as functioning as a membrane stabilizer and metabolic enhancer for nutrients to get

to the brain. It is also a source of cellular energy. Although CoQ10 is found in animal foods, the amounts digested do not approach therapeutic requirements.

3. L-theanine (5-N-ethylglutamine) has been used in instances of trauma or periods of severe stress. The result of taking this substance is the promotion of a restful, relaxed state without diminishing daytime alertness. Biologically it has been shown to increase serotonin and/or dopamine concentrations in the brain. Both chemicals lead to well-being and a positive mood. It also has been used to delay nerve death during periods in which the brain is undergoing confusion and insults (psychological or physical). These symptoms are prevalent in Asperger's and autistic syndromes. This substance has been found in green tea.

4. Carnosine is a natural substance that has been used to foster frontal lobe function (increased attention and focus) and has a brain protective function. Individuals with autistic features have been shown to improve in vocabulary and organization, which would show promise for other people with neurological issues in these areas. Interestingly, the literature suggests that this substance also possesses neurotransmission activity that modulates enzymatic activities, such as chelating heavy metals.

5. The combination of American ginseng (200 mg) and ginkgo biloba (50 mg) has been shown to yield significant improvement in hyperactive-impulsive behaviors as well as improving high anxiety or shy traits related to social problems. There has also been improvement in performances of quality of memory at the highest dose and speed of attention at a mid-dose range.

6. Ginkgo biloba in daily doses of 120 to 240 mg can improve symptoms of memory loss, depression, and tinnitus (ringing in the ears), especially if the symptoms are related to trauma. It serves as a free-radical scavenger (which is a major aid in prevention of disease) but may have direct effects on the cholinergic system. This may explain its positive impact on acute and chronic cognitive deficits. The benefits appear to have drawn a host of supporters; however, it must be emphasized that you should buy pharmaceutical

quality of this product. Because this is not a government-certified substance, as many as 30 percent of the products available do not contain any amounts of ginkgo biloba, despite the labels' claims, and as many as 20 percent contain only trace amounts. With that caution, the attributes of this substance alone have demonstrated these benefits:

• Improvement of memory performance

• Improvement of learning capacity

• Improvement in compensation for disturbed equilibrium

• Inactivation of toxic radicals

• Neuroprotective effect (brain shield)

• Relaxation effect

7. American ginseng (*Panax quinquefolius*) has been documented to enhance central nervous system activity (brain and spinal cord), decrease fatigue, and increase motor activity. Ginseng has antidepressant, antipsychotic, anticonvulsant, analgesic, antipyretic, and ulcer-protective qualities. It has been shown to inhibit conditions such as anxiety and depression. Interestingly related to toxicity, it has an anti-inflammatory quality and increases gastrointestinal action, thereby decreasing constipation. When taken in combination with *Panax ginseng* (Chinese ginseng), it was found to greatly reduce concentration problems and symptoms of attention deficit disorder. *Panax ginseng* has been shown to have beneficial effects on the immune cells of individuals with chronic fatigue syndrome, an affliction associated with individuals with attention deficit disorder as well as autism.

NATURAL APPROACHES TO CLEANSING THE BRAIN

Mentioned in the beginning of this chapter were possible infestations of parasites and their adverse effects on your overall health. If you want to get concerned about how your colon is dealing with your environment, I suggest that you read an article in the August 2000 issue of *Discovery* magazine, "Do Parasites Rule the World?" by Carl Zimmer, that warned, "Every living thing has at least one parasite that lives within it." It might scare you to see the awful-looking creatures that live within a person's body.

It might also inspire you to visit your doctor and have a stool sample analysis to rule out any possible problems from such visitors. Most people who go through a colon cleansing as a routine process give terrific testimonies about how their lives have changed as a result. An Internet search for natural detox of the colon (or liver) will yield hundreds of such testimonies and products that foster such beliefs.

I do not know exactly what supplements work for everyone or individually, but this is a list of the ingredients that have been found to help the cleansing process:

- Flaxseed

- Fennel seed

- Licorice root

- Aloe vera

- Grapefruit pectin

- Papaya fruit

- Slippery elm bark

- Marshmallow root

- Rhubarb root

- Alfalfa

- Guar gum

- Peppermint

- Ginger tea

In addition to the benefits of natural supplements for the reduction of nasty contaminants in your body, there are some old and even ancient methods that work, especially against water-soluble poisons. These aid the body in eliminating toxins through sweat glands, urine, and other natural processes. My own investigations have found that tremendous numbers of people have seen improvements through these remedies, particularly among Native American and East Indian populations, but they are less commonly used in Western medicine. Nevertheless, these are listed for your consideration.

- Hot saunas, especially with sesame or juniper oils

- Physical exercise

- Massages, especially when performed by massage specialists who know how to help the lymph glands release their reserves

- Lemon water

- Very high fiber diets

- Coffee enemas

Carl

Carl, seven, an unusually good-looking boy with very bright parents, had been diagnosed with mild autism when he was two years old. This diagnosis was based on his poor social skills, difficult behavior, and poor learning skills. While Carl was very proficient in some areas, he was hindered by a lack of effective communication, and showed ritualistic infantile motor behavior, such as clapping hands and rocking motions when he was nervous. He was unable to sit still long enough to have a QEEG brain scan, so we administered the biological tests for toxicity. The results were startling.

Carl's body had lead levels that were twenty-four times what is considered acceptable. We were surprised that he was functional at all. Six months of chelation, based on the DMSA approach, brought his levels down significantly and his behavior changed accordingly. He was able to process information much more readily, but he still maintained his rebellious nature. We had to work with him and his family for six more months to find effective behavioral management. At last report, he is with his age group in school and adjusting to a "normal way of life."

I mention Carl's story for two reasons.

One: To demonstrate that children can have very high metal exposure even if they are living in a "clean" environment.

Two: Even when the toxicity is withdrawn from the brain, if there has been some history in which compensation behaviors have been adopted for anxiety and stress, you may have to start at that point for adjustment therapy. This is not to say that behavioral problems will exist permanently, but when a child is assaulted with this kind of injury at a young age, he or she will still need to learn more effective choices for behavioral consequences. The good news is that the "cleansed" child will have the mental resources to make the adjustments.

THE NEXT STEP

Scientists have only recently become alert to the fact that brain toxicity can be a major source of cognitive problems ranging from poor concentration to chronic pain perceptions. This is an exciting advance for modern medicine. I have no doubt that brain toxicity is a contributing factor in other issues, such as postwar trauma and worker productivity. I believe that many, many people can improve their lives and attain new levels of accomplishment by making some relatively simple adjustments. If you can't tap into your full brainpower, you can expect to struggle psychologically, physiologically, and even spiritually. You need the full function of this vital organ. In this chapter, I've given you examples and direction on how to recharge your system and redirect your life. But we're not done yet! So keep the oxygen flowing and your brain growing by reading on!

Four

NURTURING YOUR INTELLECT THROUGH BRAIN FUEL

Adults tend to shudder at the prospect of dealing with troubled teens. I love them. The challenges are stimulating, and the rewards are incredible. I have worked with adolescents most of my career. Troubled teens, particularly those struggling to make it in school because of alcohol or drug abuse, are my specialty. Often, others label them misfits while they, in turn, adopt the role of victims scorned by the "popular crowd."

Typically, teens with drug and alcohol problems are directed into some version of the tried and true 12-step program long used for addicts and alcoholics. I've got to admit, I went with the program as a treatment method early in my career. I saw it as a very viable way for young patients to gather strength so they could redirect their high energy levels toward more constructive goals.

But sometimes the standard model of treatment doesn't fit the realities of the situation, and a caring psychologist must adapt his or her treatments to the needs of his patients. It struck me that many kids weren't ready for the 12-step program until they'd progressed far enough along that they were capable of making critical choices for their lives. The 12-step program asks a lot of difficult questions up front. It calls for participants to evaluate their goals and deep spiritual beliefs. But we found that, often, kids with serious addictions are not ready for that sort of deep thinking. They came to us after seven days of detoxification, usually with their heads still reeling from that arduous process. Because of all the junk that had gone into their brains, there just wasn't enough time or opportunity for us to take them through one step, much less twelve. Drug and alcohol abuse becomes a disease because there is bio-logical damage that has to be restored.

Drugs and alcohol traumatize the brain and shut it down. The trauma can last for years. It is no wonder, then, that recidivism is so astoundingly high for alcoholics and addicts. It ranges from 60 percent to 90 percent in even the best of programs. Addictive substances linger in the nervous system for months. It is a very hard fight and many don't make it. In looking for ways to help the young people brought to me, I found that beating their addictions was just the preliminary step.

> Most school cafeterias are staffed by poorly trained, badly equipped workers who churn out 4.8 billion hot lunches a year. Often the meals, produced for about $1 each, consist of breaded meat patties, french fries, and overcooked vegetables. So the kids buy muffins, cookies, and ice cream—or feast on fast food from McDonald's, Pizza Hut, or Taco Bell, which are available in more than half the schools in the nation. "We're killing our kids with the food we serve," says Texas Education Commissioner Susan Combs. (*Newsweek*, August 8, 2005)

In looking at the whole person, not just the addict, I discovered that nearly all of these kids were suffering from malnutrition. It wasn't that they were not eating. In fact, most had diets right off the main menu. Breakfast usually contained a choice of cereals, fruits, doughnuts or pas-tries, oatmeal and toast. Lunch was likely to be sandwiches, hot dogs, or fried chicken. Dinner was usually not prepared because they rarely ate what was served at home. Most went with pizza, hamburgers, milk shakes, or whatever they could order up. This may seem like the typical teen diet, but addicts are not typical in any way. You can imagine the shock and dismay from my teen patients when I took over the kitchen and turned the menus upside down with Dr. Frank's eating program. For breakfast, they had a choice of boiled eggs, toast with all-natural peanut butter, cottage cheese with fruit, skimmed milk and/or coffee. For lunch, I offered them tuna, tomatoes, bananas, and a high protein bar. Dinner selections included cooked carrots, a baked potato, fruit-flavored yogurt, steak or grilled chicken.

My patients were peeved about my interference in their diets. But I made my views known. They were not hotel guests. They were my re-sponsibility and I was going to treat them according to what they needed, not what they craved. I told them that I believed in them and that I thought they were smart kids who weren't making smart choices. I told them that if they were to make lives for themselves they had to fuel up properly to achieve their goals.

It took about three days for them to see the light, or at least to start feeling healthier as the toxins were cleansed from their systems. At that point, we started making huge progress. Their cravings disappeared, and they felt energized. A few of them even started a band. Their minds were filled with creative thoughts. As we say in tweedy, pipe-smoking psychiatrist circles, they rocked!

I still get letters from some of those former troubled teens. Both they and I experienced rewards from our time together. Not one of these teens returned to drugs. I believe the program worked because once we treated their addictions we introduced them to proper nutrition, which allowed them to get their brains and bodies back in harmony. We gave them the strength to find their greatest potential.

ASSESSMENT

While it is true that brain dysfunctions have many sources, nutrition is a major consideration. There's brain food and then there is *brain-drain* food. To assess whether you are functioning to your full potential, take the following evaluation. These items are designed to reveal a nutritional imbalance. Answer whether or not you experience what is described by noting if it is true all the time (T), true some of the time (ST), or never true (N).

1. There are times in the day when I feel weak and have great loss of energy.

    T   ST   N

2. I crave sugar or sweets during the day.

    T   ST   N

3. I feel depressed except when I get excited about something or my mind is diverted to a special interest.

   T   ST   N

4. I am forgetful, especially in the morning.

   T   ST   N

5. I have a high-sugar breakfast and am hungry the rest of the day.

   T   ST   N

6. I wear glasses to read or see long distances.

   T   ST   N

7. I have trouble concentrating.

   T   ST   N

8. I have trouble falling asleep.

   T   ST   N

9. I am stressed most of the time, but I can't figure out what I am stressed about.

   T   ST   N

10. Although I am thirsty, I drink little water each day, just what I get in colas and other prepared drinks.

    T   ST   N

11. I am very sensitive to drugs or alcohol.

    T   ST   N

12. I get obsessive in my worrying and thinking of bad things that could happen to me or my loved ones.

    T   ST   N

13. I have irrational fears that have no basis.

    T   ST   N

14. I have stomachaches and other digestive tract problems, such as constipation or diarrhea.

    T   ST   N

15. I feel that I am aging faster than I should.

    T   ST   N

16. My joints and muscles ache.

    T   ST   N

17. I have mood swings almost every day.

    T   ST   N

18. My moods and attitudes seem always to be different from others', and I get irritated with these differences.

    T   ST   N

19. Often I find fried foods to be the only things I can eat or like, even if there are more nutritious foods available.

    T   ST   N

20. My energy is limited and I feel weak quickly.

    T   ST   N

Scoring:

Give credit of two (2) to each T and one (1) to each ST. Total your score and consider that any score over 4 should lead you to consider nutrition as an important part of your mental potential, and any score over 10 is a strong indicator that you are in serious need of a nutritional consultation in order to prevent major mental limitations.

A NUTRITIONAL PLAN IN REVERSE TO EMPOWER THE BRAIN

Poor nutrition and its impact on our overall health are major concerns even in our affluent American society. Diet gurus consistently condemn sugars and/or fats. The public is often confused by the conflicting information over what is healthy and what is not. Cardiologists argue over the best prevention for heart disease. Doctors and dietitians treating diabetes rarely agree on nutritional protocol. Diabetic groups often call for better education about food ingredients. Some claim certain foods trigger violent tendencies.

There is evidence that highly processed foods contribute to health problems. I'm a champion of healthier foods for healthier living. I am concerned that far too many contaminants get into our food supply. You are what you eat. So you shouldn't let anyone feed you horse meat, sawdust, or rodent or bug feces.

Sorry. Didn't mean to gross you out. But what you don't know can hurt you. And you can be seriously hurt by what you eat unknowingly. Our dietary problems aren't new. And they include such staples of our diet as sugar, the white gold that we've been consuming since the early 1700s. Aristocrats craved sugar and they forced slaves to produce it for them. Early pioneers in nutrition and medicine recognized that ill-advised foods like sugar and certain animal products might be responsible for health problems. In the early 1900s, they set up special spas and clinics to encourage better nutrition as a treatment for health problems. Dr. John Kellogg was one of those pioneers. He set up a leading nutrition center in Battle Creek, Michigan, where patients came for help with obesity and related diseases. Dr. Kellogg, as you might guess, advocated cereal as a health food. (This was way before Froot Loops and Count Chocula hit the market.)

One of Kellogg's patients, C. W. Post, got the idea of coating cereals with sugar. The taste improved. Post Toasties was one of the first Post cereals to hit it big. Dr. Kellogg's brother, W. K. Kellogg, took it to the next level and poured on the sugary coatings. It was great for business, but bad for the typical American diet.

Sylvester Graham was another Victorian-era nutritional advocate. He believed in temperance and vegetables. He suspected, wisely, that sugar, alcohol, and animal fats put a strain on the brain. He invented a "cookie" of unsifted ground wheat, later known as the "graham cracker," that became very popular. But this, too, was corrupted with sugar and preservatives that made it an unhealthy choice.

Both cereals and graham crackers were well-intentioned, nutritional foods that were turned into unhealthy choices. They are typical in that regard. So many good foods are transformed into bad foods by corrupting influences somewhere along the food chain. No wonder we are a nation—and increasingly a world—of junk-food junkies. Over the last fifty years, we have increased our consumption of carbonates and decreased consumption of healthy proteins because of bad choices. We are paying the price for those bad dietary choices.

Sugar is a natural ingredient. Yet we consume it in unhealthy quantities, and often in unnatural forms, that make it difficult for the body to process it in a healthy manner. This is true of all natural substances. Potatoes are a natural food. Fried potatoes in the form of french fries are not a natural food.

Let's say that you started the day eating jelly doughnuts washed down with orange juice. Remember that your body has been away from food for ten to twelve hours while you slept (hopefully), so you are breaking a fast (hence the term—breakfast). With the doughnuts and the orange juice, you have introduced a huge amount of sugar into your bloodstream. Your body isn't made to handle that kind of sugar load. It sends your blood sugar soaring and disrupts the normal function of your kidneys and even your blood vessels. The body's natural response to this unnatural sugar load is to produce insulin.

Insulin is the substance that binds with the blood sugar and helps transport it into the organs, muscles, and brain for use. Without the help of insulin, the blood sugar would just pool in the bloodstream and cause all kinds of problems, which is what happens in diabetes. When you are introducing sugar into your system at a high rate, the insulin from your pancreas is pumping at full steam trying to diminish the amount of blood sugar to safe levels. Often, your poor pancreas can't keep up.

That's not a good thing. When the pancreas falls behind in trying to deal with sugar in your system, your insulin level goes up and down like a roller coaster for the rest of the day. Yet, by starting out with a more "natural" meal with a balance of sugar and protein, you give your body the fuel it needs without overtaxing it. You won't get a "sugar high" when you eat a balanced meal. The sugar high triggers huge changes in energy levels and brain power. Twenty minutes after you eat, the high flow of insulin generated transports the blood sugar to your organs. But any excess insulin produced also wipes out your reserve blood sugar, sending your system into a dive. This is called the hypoglycemic response. It is nothing to mess around with. People who are particularly sensitive can go into comas.

Since your brain does not store sugar but requires more of it than any other organ in your body, it runs out of fuel during the hypoglycemic response. As a result, you may not remember your own name. Or, as my writing mentor, Dr. Maggie Robinson, says, "If you don't eat good protein in the morning, pretty soon you start leaving out topic sentences."

It doesn't help when you respond to low blood sugar by dumping more unnatural levels of it into your screwed-up system. When you stumble across the room and wolf down a Snickers you do get another rush, but it's only the first dip on the new roller-coaster ride. At some point, you have to get off the ride. If you continue to stress your pancreas, it may fail. Then you are looking at a high probability of diabetes and heart disease, both of which can lead to permanent brain damage.

I like a Snickers as much as anyone. But if you understand how sugar works in the body, you'll see why moderation in Snickers consumption is a wise choice. High heat converts protein and other substances into sugar. That is why the fat from the steak you eat becomes a type of sugar inside the body. Even cigarette tobacco is transformed into a sugar once it enters the bloodstream. Eating too much of anything, even protein, will cause the body to reach its maximum and begin to turn protein into blood sugar.

PRESERVATIVES THAT PUT OUR BRAINS IN NEUTRAL GEAR

There are other nutritional issues that block the foods we eat from becoming useful fuels for our bodies. Preservatives are often added to foods to increase their shelf life. But preservatives impair the body's ability to break down foods for consumption.

I do not want to start a war with the food industry. But I want you to fulfill your potential as a human being, and to do that, you have to eat wisely.

THE SEVEN MAGIC INGREDIENTS FOR MENTAL MUSCLE

There are seven major "foods" that are essential for your brain's optimal performance. Some of them will seem fairly basic, but there is nothing common about common sense, so they bear repeating. And you may be surprised at the current science on some of these "basic" brain foods. Take a look but don't take my word for it. Do your own tests with these foods and supplements and others that you may wish to try.

1. Water

I realize that this ingredient is not very sexy, although it often comes in a pretty bottle at a steep price. Nevertheless, water deserves respect as a major stimulator for neurotransmission in the brain. While there are obvious differences in water composition (sources, minerals, etc.), no one kind of water appears to hold the edge in intelligence improvement. I'll leave it to your personal preferences when it comes to taste and purity.

I will caution you that tap water in some areas is saturated with fluoride. Fluoride makes your body absorb aluminum faster, and one of the most deadly metals associated with brain dysfunction is aluminum. There is a major correlation of aluminum consumption with Alzheimer's and other types of dementia. While many people don't care to consume large quantities of water, there are ways to make it more appealing. Lemon and light quantities of natural juices can help make it more palatable. My recommendation is to drink half your body weight in ounces. If you weigh 150 pounds, then your daily water intake should be 75 ounces, which is roughly five half-litre bottles a day.

2. Natural carbohydrates

The key word is "natural." As noted earlier, too much unnatural sugar messes up the balance of your metabolism and drains your brain of energy. Natural carbohydrates include whole grains, fruits, and vegetables. Do not heat these before eating them. A fried tomato is not a tomato anymore. It has been chemically altered by the heat, and the extra sugar released does more harm than good.

3. Antioxidants

To keep it simple, you only need to understand that when the brain is insulted by things like alcohol and cigarette smoke, "free radicals" are released. These free-ranging agents keep the body from using oxygen efficiently. Things go haywire in a process known as *oxidation* and the results are not beneficial. You can see this reaction in other forms by observing the rust that forms on iron, or the spoiling of food.

Because the brain consumes more oxygen than any other organ in the body, it is especially vulnerable to oxidation. To protect your brain, you need to consume antioxidants. The chief vitamin antioxidants are vitamin C, vitamin E, vitamin B_6, and vitamin B_{12}. Others include selenium, zinc, calcium, and magnesium.

> The benefit of vitamin B_6 in a variety of health issues is well documented. Pure vitamin B_6 cannot enter the brain, however, because a wall of resistance to some supplements with toxins prevents them from passing into the brain region. A form of B_6 in a supplement called P5P can pass through the brain barrier, and thereby support neurological health.

Direct supplements can be used to develop an antioxidant army. Here are general guidelines on daily dosages. Please note that they vary according to your age, weight, and individual needs. Consult with a specialist to determine your particular needs. If you want to increase your brainpower even more, you can probably safely double the dosages—but, again, consult your nutrition specialist.

ANTIOXIDANT SUPPLEMENTS

Vitamin C	250 mg daily
Vitamin E	200 IU daily
Alpha-lipoic Acid	20–50 mg daily
Vitamin B_6	50 mg daily
Vitamin B_{12}	50 mcg daily
Calcium	260 mg
Magnesium	160 mg daily

The pure form of ascorbic acid can reach the brain through the brain barrier more efficiently than its lesser form, vitamin C.

Supplements have been shown to increase various functions, but real food is still the best way to get nutrients. Therefore, I recommend the following foods as major suppliers of antioxidants:

- Beets

- Red grapes

- Berries, especially blueberries and raspberries

- Red peppers

- Spinach

- Prunes

- Citrus fruits

- Sweet potatoes

- Carrots

- Tomatoes

- Onions

- Broccoli

- Asparagus

- Cabbage

- Brussels sprouts

- Beans

- Watermelon

- Wheat germ

- Nuts

4. Omega-3 fats

These are the stars of brain foods. They are more commonly known as fatty acids or "good fats." The term "omega" refers to the classification of the kind of fat, and this kind of fat is what the brain and the neurons use for their insulation. These fats are good because they increase the speed of nerve impulses and connections. Omega-3 fats also combat depression, enhance learning and memory, and serve as major aids to brain plasticity (re-creating brain structures for efficiency of neuron transmission).

> About 25 percent of the population has a genetic predisposition for carrying Alzheimer's disease. They carry the E4 form of the lipoprotein apoE. People who carry this gene also have been found to have low levels of vitamin K. Calcification and the development of lesions in blood vessels that feed the brain tissues are believed to be a component of Alzheimer's development. Further research may reveal high-dose vitamin K therapy to be preventive. (Allergy Research Group newsletter, June 2005)

You can buy omega-3 oils in health food stores. There are no confirmed side effects. I highly recommend "krill oil," which is taken from shrimp and other sea life. In food, omega-3 fats come in three varieties:

alpha-linolenic acid (ALA), eicosapentaenoic acid (EPA), and docosa-hexaenoic acid (DHA). ALA is found mostly in plant foods such as flax, soybeans, and vegetables. These substances are converted into EPA and DHA in the body. EPA and DHA are found in fish, where they are preformed. Just a four-once portion of salmon twice a week serves about five grams of omega-3, the amount recommended for brain food.

Not all fish produce these quantities of omega-3 fats, so this table offers relative production for your needs.

Top omega-3 fish per ounce*

- Sardines   3.3 g
- Mackerel   2.5 g
- Salmon   1.8 g
- Herring   1.7 g
- Bluefin tuna   1.6 g
- Lake trout   1.6 g

5. Folic acid

This nutrient is one of three B complex vitamins (B_6 and B_{12} are the others) that reduce and battle a brain- and heart-damaging protein called *homocysteine*. It is an amino acid that injures the inner walls of your arteries, causing them to thicken and narrow. Homocysteines contribute to cardiovascular problems that can lead to strokes, depression, dementia, and possibly even Alzheimer's disease.

You can buy folic acid as well as vitamins B_6 and B_{12} in most health food stores. It also can be obtained from dark-green leafy vegetables. Lima beans, cauliflower, beef, eggs, and nuts also supply folic acid.

---

*Adapted from Nettle, J. A. 1991. Omega-3 Fatty acids: Comparison of plant and seafood sources. *Journal of the American Dietetic Assn.* 91:331–337.

6. Thiamine (Vitamin B₁)

This substance helps manufacture acetylcholine, one of the brain's primary messengers. It triggers a metabolism process that helps the brain better use the food available to it. Even if you eat only "healthy" food, if it lacks B_1 there is little gain. Nuts and whole grains are stockpiles of this substance.

7. Vitamin D

This is the sunshine vitamin, but many individuals are in the dark about it. Vital to the brain and a possible factor in fending off Alzheimer's, vitamin D is critical to maintaining the ratio of calcium to phosphorus. It helps transport calcium in and out of bones. The hippocampus is a major memory center in the brain and is very sensitive to this valuable vitamin.

Vitamin D is manufactured by the interaction of sun rays and the skin. Couch potatoes, video game junkies, and television zombies all risk a lack of vitamin D.

STRATEGIC NUTRITIONAL PLAN FOR COGNITIVE CONNECTIONS

The substances and supplements I've listed are recommended for general mental improvement. For specific mental improvement, I've got some other ideas for optimizing your performance. These supplements can tune your brain to high "smart" frequencies to improve mental acuity. A note of caution: No one knows how these fuels work in combination. Some may cancel out others. Certain other common remedies, such as anti-inflammatories, may also interfere with their effectiveness.

Memory is an intellectual function that is integrated with other processes. It can be accessed in various parts of the brain. It also plays a special role in storing information and integrating it. This function is critical for learning new information that helps you meet new challenges. Memory is also the brain function that is most often tested as a measure of general intelligence. You can boost memory with natural foods like bananas and even chocolate, or, for double the recall, try chocolate-covered bananas. The most important thing when choosing memory boosters is how efficiently the body processes them. Below is a list of supplements that will offer you more efficiency in these realms.

1. Acetyl-L-carnitine (dosage up to 1,000 mg a day) has been shown to promote the activity of two neurotransmitters, acetylcholine and dopamine, both of which promote clearer thinking patterns. These neurotransmitters improve the communication among the parts of the brain, which improves creativity and higher-level problem solving. They also improve reflex speed and accuracy, which is very important for us older folks.

2. Alpha-glycerylphosphosphorylcholine (alpha-GPC) (dosage 400 mg three times daily) is rich in choline, the major player in intelligence. It combines glycerol and phosphate, which protect the brain cell membranes. This brainpower booster has been documented to improve intelligence test–taking skills, especially those measuring memory. It also appears to have amazing recuperative properties for stroke patients in the areas of intellectual functioning.

3. *Bacopa monniera* (Brahmi) is an Indian plant used for five thousand years to treat stress and boost intellectual stimulation. Clinical evidence of the human benefits is scant, but studies on rats demonstrate improved learning capacities and significantly improved memories. Chances are you are not a rat, but the theory holds that this substance works by regenerating dendrites (nerve connecting cells) and boosting production of serotonin in the brain. Rats and people might want to note that this plant contains a substance resembling the poison strychnine, so sticking with the recommended dosages—70 mg of the extract twice a day—is a good move.

4. Choline (dosage 1,500 mg daily) is widely applauded as a mental stimulant. It is produced within your body from two amino acids, methionine and serine, with help from vitamin B_{12} and folic acid.

As a supplement it can have a very powerful impact on your performance in IQ tests.

5. *Ginkgo biloba* (dosage 120–240 mg three times daily) is my favorite supplement for a very nonscientific reason. It works great for me. Chances are, it'll work well for you too. It is believed to enhance blood supply to the brain while also decreasing inflammations. It stimulates the memory and problem-solving areas of the brain.

6. Ginseng is probably the herb most hyped for promoting good health and mental alertness, but you should be very careful about where you get it. As discussed earlier, there are reports of some unethical suppliers out there. Be sure you get the pharmaceutical-level quality from a reputable supplier. Ginseng is beneficial because it contains ginsenosides, which stimulate the brain's neurotransmitters so that it can synthesize proteins optimally. In one study, college students who took *Panax ginseng* showed more improvement in mental acuity than students who took nothing. In other tests of the herb, proofreaders functioned at higher levels while using it. Older adults have been shown to benefit greatly from ginseng. A study of 256 people (aged forty to sixty-six) showed an average of 7 percent improvement on computerized recall, recognition, and spatial tests. Subjects took 200 mg of ginseng with 120 mg of ginkgo.

Your brainpower will also improve if you eat foods that increase your levels of protein through the day. Protein-rich foods supply tyrosine, which increases alertness as well as endurance in cognitive tasks. Sample menus for meals or snacks are presented below:

Menu 1: Omelet (two eggs, cheese, chopped green pepper, onion and tomato)

One slice whole wheat or whole grain toast

One cup of Concord grape juice

One cup coffee or tea

Menu 2: 4 ounces grilled chicken salad
(2–3 cups of salad vegetables, one tomato)

Coffee or tea

Menu 3: Deviled eggs:

Three eggs (hard boiled)

Plain yogurt

Mustard

One tablespoon pickle relish

Salt and pepper

Menu 4: 4–5 ounces grilled shrimp

Sweet potato (steamed or baked)

Skim milk

Menu 5: One tin sardines

Triscuits or other whole wheat crackers

Mustard

Menu 6: Fruit salad

Sliced strawberries

Mango

Banana

Low-fat vanilla yogurt

2–3 tablespoons wheat germ

Notes:

- Apples, pears, almonds, and tomatoes are loaded with boron, which gives additional power for attention and memory.

- Coffee and tea are sources of caffeine, which, in moderation, gives more energy for mental activities.

- Leafy greens found in salads provide high levels of potassium, which is a major factor in concentration.

- Grape juice, sweet potatoes, and other vegetables are major antioxidants.

STRATEGIC NUTRITIONAL PLAN FOR MOOD ENERGY

Your mood reflects your mental energy. When you shut down emotionally, your brain shuts down intellectually. Conflicts and challenges rock everyone's world. It is all too easy to make yourself miserable with worry. You can't control what happens to you or in the world around you but you can control your attitude. But sometimes your mood goes dark because the lights are dim somewhere inside your brain. If your brain is not getting what it needs to function properly, depression can result. Mood-enhancing substances that treat breakdowns in the brain are available.

1. Gamma-aminobutyric acid (GABA) (dosage 200 mg taken four times a day) is an amino acid that appears to prevent the transmission of anxiety messages from nerve cell to nerve cell. This is an anxiety management agent that neutralizes stress and serves as a powerful relaxing agent without sacrificing alertness.

2. Glutamine (dosage 0.5–5 g daily) is another amino acid that is converted into glutamic acid in your brain. The glutamic acid serves as a building block for proteins and nucleotides (RNA and DNA) that stimulate your brain in the mood regions as well as elevating the GABA levels for stress management. This substance is very important to relieve mental fatigue.

- The discovery of nitric oxide is a huge benefit for cognitive functioning. Perhaps the most important element yet found for regulation of all our bodies' functions, nitric oxide plays a major role in the development of neuron-to-neuron signaling and contributes to the formation of memory. Used by the firefly for its luminance, this substance can actually light up your brain. (*No More Heart Disease* by Dr. Louis J. Ignarro)
- Supplements that can enhance nitric oxide within your system:
    L-arginine 4–6 grams daily
    L-citrulline 200–1,000 mg daily
    Vitamin C 500 mg daily
    Vitamin E 200 IU daily
    Folic acid (vitamin B_9) 400–800 mcg daily
    Alpha-lipoic acid 10 mg daily
(Dr. Louis J. Ignarro, Nobel laureate in medicine for the discovery of nitric oxide)

3. Phenylalanine is another building block for brain neurotransmitters that works directly with depression and sadness. It is also helpful with memory and alertness, and can provide a real boost, like an amphetamine lift in spirit and libido. Phenylalanine can be found in almonds, avocados, bananas, cheese, cottage cheese, dried milk (nonfat), chocolate, pumpkin seeds, and sesame seeds. Supplementally, phenylalanine comes in three forms: L-phenylalanine (found in food), D-phenylalanine (not found in food), and DL-phenylalanine (combination). The L-phenylalanine is used mostly for mood, while the DL-phenylalanine has been used for Parkinson's disease and alertness. There are many precautions for using this substance with other drugs. It's also wise to be careful with certain physical conditions, such as hypertension, diabetes, and migraine. The recommended dosages are 500–1,000 mg daily. As always, consult your physician before beginning any new supplement regimen.

4. Tyrosine, a building block of several neurotransmitters, including dopamine, norepinephrine, and epinephrine, is synthesized from phenylalanine. Interestingly, depression is associated with low

levels of tyrosine and low levels of dopamine, *which have also been indicated as major factors in Parkinson's disease.* Tyrosine is a natural component in food, such as dairy products, meat, fish, wheat, oats, bananas, and seeds. As a supplement, label dosages range from 500 to 2,000 mg two to three times daily.

5. 5-hydroxytryptamine (5-HT), a close cousin to tryptophan, is a known precursor to serotonin, the neurotransmitter highly related to depression, anxiety, stress, and other moods of low mental energy. The general recommended dosages are 100 to 300 mg, three times daily. Be cautious if you are taking medications for certain conditions, such as depression, heart disease, or blood pressure.

MAJOR FOODS THAT AFFECT MOOD

Food doesn't always cure the blues, but eating the right stuff can improve your mood. If you've been crying so hard your spurs are rusting, don't reach for the whiskey bottle or the chocolate doughnuts. Instead, tap into those healthier foods that can do you some serious good. These can be very helpful with your mood, as well as being healthful for your body, which is quite a breakthrough.

Brazil nuts

These tasty mega-nuts are packed with selenium, a major player on the antioxidant team. Selenium works to protect the brain against toxins. Toxins can and do create turmoil in the brain that causes mood swings. Brazil nuts come packed with high levels of selenium but you can also get big doses of it from tuna, lean meat, organ meats, chicken, cottage cheese, fruit, and whole grains.

Milk

"Nature's own" soft drink is rich in calcium, which offers many benefits to the body. It can be useful in weight management and in treating cardiovascular problems. A study of milk's effects on women with premenstrual syndrome (PMS) at Mount Sinai reported that a whopping 75 percent experienced less irritability, nervousness, and depression after drinking milk. Milk has also been credited with pain reduction. Other foods with high calcium content include orange juice (calcium fortified), tofu, low-fat yogurt, and turnip greens.

Fish

Omega-3, which is found in fish, is considered a brain food and a mood booster. Fish contains high levels of serotonin, which is also found in shrimp, oysters, and crabs.

Turkey

This old favorite contains tyrosine and natural tryptophan. These substances relieve anxiety and stress while also tending to make you sleepy after Thanksgiving dinner, especially when combined with boring in-laws.

Beef

Red meat doesn't get a lot of respect these days but I give it good marks for mood enhancement, probably because of the high levels of iron (which reduces fatigue) and selenium.

Whole-grain breads

Hold the butter, but give bread a break as a source of good nutrition with grains that contain high levels of amino acids, which synthesize brain fuels.

Chocolate

In some cases, this candy is dandy. Dark chocolate has mental enhancing properties that improve mood. It contains theobromine, a mental stimulant closely related to caffeine. Phenylethylamine (PEA) is another ingredient in chocolate. It is considered to be an aphrodisiac, which spawns a form of energy thought by Freud to be the source of all power. Dark chocolate also includes anandamine, which acts much like tetrahydrocannabinol (THC), the active ingredient in marijuana, in aiding relaxation.

Cinnamon

This is a great spice because it has no calories even though it is a major taste stimulant. It is also a big aid in treating hypoglycemia (low blood sugar). Cinnamon contains a compound, methylhydroxy chalcone polymer (MHCP), that improves the body's management of blood sugar.

Spinach

Maybe Popeye was right. You, too, can be strong to the finish if you "eats" your spinach! Spinach is loaded with vitamin B folic acid that is effective in treating depression and increasing your mental energy levels.

Honey

The bees are on to something. Their food is loaded with natural tryptophan for serotonin, the happiness transmitter.

Bananas

Some of my patients think I own stock in a banana plantation because of my enthusiasm for this food. But I'm bananas about bananas because they contain magnesium, a mineral that can be depleted by stress. Bananas are also a source for tryptophan and potassium, big players in antistress treatment and pain management.

Spices

Spicy isn't always bad. Hot peppers can lower pain and heighten a sense of happiness, regardless of how much your eyes water. It is thought that the endorphin neurotransmitter network (internal morphine-like molecules) that serve as pain relievers can give a boost to pleasure centers.

SOME FINAL THOUGHTS

This chapter offers you an array of choices for eating, living, and thinking successfully. The brain needs both air and food, and you need to make certain that it gets those in healthy doses. Modern technology has brought us synthesized food and nutrition products. But you need to remember that what works for one person might not work as well for you. One size does not fit all. Moreover, an imbalance in any one substance can often cause more problems than it cures. The safest course is to eat the correct balance, and to trust that nature knows best.

You are responsible for your own health and the decisions you make about what goes into your body. If you don't know the answers to your questions about healthy eating, vitamins, and supplements, you owe it to yourself to find an expert who can help you address your concerns.

Five

THE FOGGY MIND

Maria's parents looked frightened as they came into the PNP Center. They were panicked that she was not ready to graduate from high school and they were fearful that she'd never get into college. Maria struggled throughout her schooling because of her attention deficit hyperactive disorder (ADHD).

ADHD is a disorder that is marked by a poor attention span and limited concentration capacity. These often lead to poor organizational skills and difficulty remembering detailed information. Typical school curricula are not designed for a person with ADHD. Maria studied four hours for every one hour normally required. Although she was popular with her peers and very bright, Maria dreaded school. There was a sadness about her.

ADHD more commonly affects males. When girls have it, there are special considerations. It's more acceptable for boys to act out and take risks, which is a common response to ADHD. But problems in concentration are obvious signs of the problem in boys. It is more difficult to detect ADHD in girls, and I believe they are more devastated when they perform poorly in the classroom.

Maria was a small teen with long black hair who offered a dazzling smile when I spoke to her. She dressed in revealing clothing and had multiple ear piercings. In short, she was a pretty typical high school girl. She did not show rebellious disregard for her parents and their concerns when we spoke with them. She appeared to be interested in any solutions or observations offered by my staff and me.

When I interviewed her, Maria was animated about her challenges in school. She looked directly into my eyes and said, "I have to work almost full-time to pass a high school history class. How can I pass a college course? I want to go to college and major in media communications. That is my dream. Can I do it? Can you show me how to do it?"

Without a second's hesitation I said, "Yes, you can make it, and I can coach you on how."

I said that in good faith. I believe that when someone is capable of dreaming up a goal, it is within their reach if they tap into the full power of their brains.

Maria didn't believe a word I said.

"How can you be so sure? You don't know me and you don't know my intelligence or anything. You are just trying to make me feel good, aren't you?"

I replied, "No, I am not trying to make you feel good because that would be dishonest for both of us, but I have been making judgments on people for thirty-five years. I think you can accomplish your goals, and I don't know what the plan will be yet, but we will before you finish here."

We did hours of assessment on Maria, including an intelligence test, QEEG brain scans, concentration tests, medical tests for possible levels of toxicity, family dynamics, psychological personality tests, and a behavioral vision test. We used a type of brain scan based on how the outer brain functions. It has five basic modes: Delta, Theta, Alpha, LoBeta, and HiBeta.

ELECTROENCEPHALOGRAM (EEG) MODES OF FUNCTION

Mode	Frequency	Experience
Delta range	.5–4 Hz	Sleep
Theta range	4–8 Hz	Drowsy, hypnologic
Alpha range	8–12 Hz	Relaxed, no information processing
LoBeta range	12–16 Hz	Concentration, problem solving
HiBeta range	16 Hz +	Frustration, stress

As the table shows, when the brain or a portion of the brain is in the Delta range, it is sleeping. When it is in the Theta frequency, we are experiencing a semiawake state, called the hypnologic state, where realities blend and we associate different images easily. In the Alpha range, we are relaxed and not really processing much information. In the LoBeta range, the brain begins to concentrate and process information most easily, but the brain can get too stressed when elevated to the HiBeta range, which is where we begin to overthink things with no real solutions, fretting and worrying obsessively.

Maria's brain map resembled the maps below:

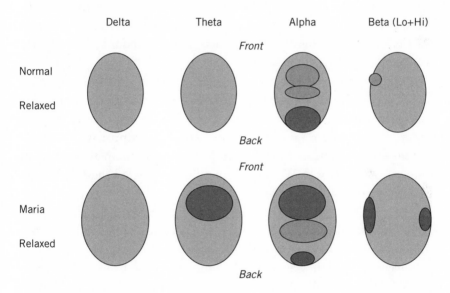

These maps are not the kind you would see on a sophisticated QEEG readout, but they serve my point. Each of the four sets of readings measures the intensity of that particular frequency (the darker the shade, the more intense that frequency). Maria was in a relaxed state of mind with her eyes open during her tests, so the frequencies of Alpha were the highest and more shaded. But the clues to Maria's challenges were found in the Theta range. We could see a darker area in the frontal lobe registering in the Theta range: the signature pattern for ADHD.

The Theta frequency in the frontal lobe indicates a drowsy and

The greater the amount of baseline cortical activation, the less performance will be affected by fatigue during a period of sleep deprivation. This study was based on pilots' performances under stress of minimum sleep conditions. (*Behavioral Neuroscience* 119, no. 3 [2005]). This means that the busier your brain is and the more it works, the less it is affected by stress and distraction.

semiconscious state. The area, devoted to problem solving, appears to be barely functioning. The lights are on but nobody is home. ADHD kids are drawn to high-risk behavior because it stimulates their drowsy brains. Maria's brain map also showed little Beta frequencies at the sides of her brain. This indicates anxiety, possibly about her frustrations in school.

Maria's brain map gave us a blueprint for treatment to improve her school performance. We wanted to find ways of waking up her brain in a constructive manner. We concentrated all of our efforts to jump-start this region, and we used a variety of stimulations. For example, we found that certain kinds of music made her brain more alert, namely, drumming music by Brent Lewis. We used a sound device, called the BAUD, and tracked the frontal lobe activity in real time.

The results were exciting. Breathing techniques and high-protein breakfasts also helped Maria control her thought patterns. She said that she could do her homework in one-third the time, and her comprehension went up too! It was a double win. Maria used these methods of brain control to make A's her senior year in high school. The last we checked, she was a college sophomore and on the dean's list for academic excellence. Now that is mind-boggling.

DO YOU HAVE A FOGGY BRAIN?

You too might have brain parts that need to be defogged. We have identified several "foggy" thinking patterns that impair peak brain performance. I have developed this questionnaire to help you become aware of the possibility that your brain may not be operating at its highest capabilities.

Describe how the following statements best pertain to you by marking Always True (AT), Sometimes True (ST), Rarely True (RT), or Never True (NT).

1. I cannot concentrate on a single topic for long periods of time.

   AT   ST   RT   NT

2. I feel lethargic and have no energy. It feels like depression.

   AT   ST   RT   NT

3. I can't stop worrying about something, even if I know that worrying is not helping.

   AT   ST   RT   NT

4. I get very obsessive about doing things right.

   AT   ST   RT   NT

5. I can't sleep because my mind keeps ruminating about something.

   AT   ST   RT   NT

6. I am stressed all the time, and often I cannot decide what I am stressed about.

   AT   ST   RT   NT

7. My memory is getting worse and worse.

   AT   ST   RT   NT

8. I am easily distracted by other events.

   AT   ST   RT   NT

9. I have trouble shifting from one idea to another—I get stuck on one subject and can't shift my thoughts when I should.

   AT   ST   RT   NT

10. I have nightmares about some event I experienced and this interferes with my sleep.

    AT   ST   RT   NT

11. I have fears about irrational things, such as closed or open spaces.

    AT   ST   RT   NT

12. I am sad, but don't know why I am sad.

    AT   ST   RT   NT

Scoring:

Assign a score of "3" to every AT you circled, a "2" to every ST, and a "1" for every RT, and total all of the twelve items for a score from zero to 36. Compare your scores to the following ranges:

24–36   Part of your brain requires major stimulation in order for you to accomplish your goals.

18–23   Your brain needs moderate stimulation for some problems in your life.

11–17   There are some goals that you could accomplish with encouragement from stimulating methods.

0–10   It is unlikely that stimulating methods would benefit you in your goal achievements.

THE BAUD

Before I tell you about the BAUD, short for Bio-Acoustical Utilization Device, you should know that I have an emotional attachment to this little gizmo. It may not save the universe or even cure athlete's foot, but I think it's a fascinating tool. I got interested in changing brain frequencies in 1978 when working as a clinical professor in orthopedic surgery with a specialization in pain management. I was asked by the chairman of the department to set up a pain management clinic. Since pain management clinics were rare in those days, I had no real models to go by, so I used the tools I had—hypnosis, mindfulness meditation, group cathartic approaches, and a lot of inspiring talks.

Well, folks, none of them worked.

In fact, everyone in my clinic got worse. It didn't look promising for my career in this field. Today, there is ample research to document that the techniques I tried are not effective, but I figured it out back then. I became discouraged until I met Michael Harner, a scholar of shamanic studies. A shaman is a healer. In tribal cultures, shamans use natural healing techniques. In movies shamans are often portrayed as "witch doctors," but increasingly, modern science has shown that many of their methods and treatments are based in valid science, and in the psychology of healing.

I explained my dilemma to Michael and he laughed at me (he usually laughed at me a lot), and explained that the shamans used the drum to deal with pain. He taught me a basic rhythm to play and told me to see if it worked. At this point, I was willing to try anything, and I never minded dancing to the beat of a different drummer.

I bought a drum and marched into the hospital the next week. I had my patients form a circle. Then, I told them that I was going to play the drum. They had no idea what would happen. Neither did I!

After twenty minutes I stopped and all the patients agreed that their pain had eased, and their moods had improved. I was beginning to understand why Ringo always seemed like the happiest Beatle.

For the next two years, I beat the drums to find the scientific explanation for this phenomenon. I'd hook patients up to the EEG, EMG, and a variety of physiological monitors to see what these drumbeats did. The results were clear. The rhythm I was taught to beat was the same as the theta wave for the brain. When this frequency was played consistently,

In a newsletter from the American Psychological Association, Division of Clinical Neuropsychology, "An Issue Devoted to Pediatric Neuropsychology," vol. 24, no. 1 (2006), Dr. Jeffrey Halpern et al. made the observation from a review of the literature that brain function often related to ADHD when diagnosed in childhood tends to resolve itself in adolescence. This may be a result of increasing maturity and/or the child's ability to adapt to challenges. Nevertheless, repeated evaluations are highly recommended.

the brain synchronized to the drum rhythms. It was relaxing the patients and creating conditions for brain imagery and a sense of well-being.

Not only did the drum rhythms reduce pain and induce constructive imagery, they also resulted in a lower frequency (delta) that helped patients sleep. This had major implications for stressed-out individuals whose brains couldn't slow down on their own.

I had the beat. It was easy to sleep to. But the next challenge was how to drum up a way to power up the brain.

Beating a drum to a LoBeta frequency (12 to 16 beats a second) would be impossible, so I asked my electronic engineer son (T. Frank Lawlis) to construct an electronic drum to stimulate the higher brain states. We discovered that the brain actually works best with mixed frequencies. I think deejays in kids' dance clubs knew this already. It's the old *in one ear and out the other* thing. For example, listening to a frequency of 20 hertz in one ear and 32 hertz in the other ear creates the net effect of 12 hertz (32–20) in the brain because of the interference between the two.

By listening to this mind mix device and monitoring brain functions, a person can create the most effective frequencies for his or her brain. That is what we do at my PNP Center. Our mental mixer looks like a large cell phone with four control knobs. Each ear has its own volume and frequency control.

This tool is interesting because it blends high technology with ancient healing techniques. It might not be right for everyone, but we've had some exciting results with it. We are doing studies on its effectiveness in treating ADHD, addictions, and PTSD, and hope to publish the results soon. We've found that individuals with addictions to alcohol, marijuana, cocaine, and certain food groups can get relief from their cravings

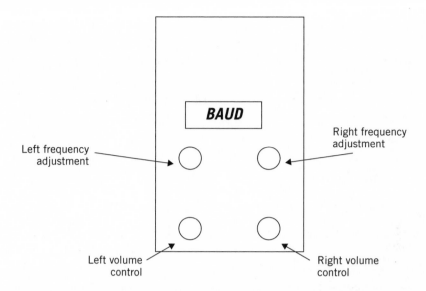

with this tool. It also helps them think more clearly. I have also had some success in relieving the tremors of a Parkinson's patient with it. I am now experimenting with combining the BAUD mix machine with vitamin C and pure oxygen, and the results look very promising for improving brain performance.

MUSIC

Music has a powerful effect on our emotions and on our brains, sometimes for better, sometimes for worse. The brain reacts to music. That's why we often feel inspired by it, or saddened by it, or just pumped up by it. There is a definite difference between your brain's response to a death march and to a parade march. That is because different kinds of music affect different portions of the brain. Gospel music that seems to trigger hopeful emotions is stimulating the amygdala, which is a very deep center in the lower cortex. That is why those who are strongly affected by gospel music might be motivated to seek a higher purpose for their lives. Interesting, sexually stimulating "mood" music also affects the lower cortex. Archeologists have found musical instruments dating back to the beginnings of human existence, and now we know why.

Relaxing music brings the brain frequencies into the alpha ranges. Sad music like Willie Nelson's profoundly moving "Half a Man" wrench the heart through the brain and feed the sadness of those listening in bars and cars. Don Campbell's excellent writings on the "Mozart effect" look at the effects of sound tones on brain function. He lists several classical pieces by Mozart (in *The Mozart Effect for Children,* 2000) that create desirable brain functions, such as the ones listed below.

For toddlers and preschoolers:

- March No. 1
- "Champagne Aria" from *Don Giovanni*
- Concertante from Serenade No. 9 in D major
- Rondo Alla Turca
- Cotillion and Allegro from Divertimento in B flat
- "Papageno's Song" from *The Magic Flute*

For schoolchildren:

- Variations from Sinfonia
- Andante from Symphony No. 6
- Andantino grazioso from Symphony No. 18
- Andantino from Symphony No. 24
- Allegro aperto from Violin Concerto No. 5 in A major
- Prestissimo from Serenade in D major
- Allegro moderato from Violin Concerto No. 2 in D major
- Andante from Symphony No. 17
- Adagio from Serenade No. 10 in B flat

His suggested musical selections do not include those associated with special brain functions and experiences. Sometimes when a patient is having problems getting out of the dumps, I have him hum or sing a song. After a few minutes, the brain responds in fascinating ways. I worked with a woman suffering from brain cancer. She was very depressed, and understandably so. I suggested she listen to music to ease her depression. She selected "Onward, Christian Soldiers" and I joined her in singing it for about twenty minutes, over and over like a mantra.

We monitored her brain and it responded to the music like a good soldier. Her depression passed. She felt confident and more optimistic about her future. The tumor even appeared to regress. Needless to say, her "Onward, Christian Soldiers" CD got a lot of play.

What is your power song? What tune might bring your brain into a more powerful state? This may be the most enjoyable therapy you ever undertake. So, fire up the iTunes, head for the music store, or even the neighborhood library's loaner collection, and find the song that sets your mind and your heart free.

PHYSICAL EXERCISE

It troubles me that psychotherapy is often seen in the Freudian stereotype of the patient lying down and talking to a therapist. The truth is that all of us think better on our feet. In fact, physical exercise is one of the best forms of therapy for stimulating brain activity. Native Americans danced around campfires when trying to solve tribal problems. As is often the case, their rituals were rooted in some solid science, even if they didn't know it. The Irish had their own methods. For centuries, people there cured depression by swimming long distances. The Chinese have traditionally performed tai chi exercises to ease and focus the mind.

Folk medicine isn't just folksy, folks. It often has a biological basis. The movement of the joints stimulates the release of endorphin neurotransmitters. That boosts the production of serotonin, which reduces depression and anxiety. An overabundance of these transmitters can create a psychological high so potent that addiction is possible. Several studies have noted that exercise can be more effective against depression than medication. Working out beats popping pills.

The added advantage of physical exercise is that it stimulates good breathing and strengthens the body. It's not a stretch at all to say that certain exercises may benefit mental and cognitive fitness too. But you should be cautious about overdoing it. You don't want to burn out your body or your brain by pushing yourself too hard. Excessive exercise can cause inflammation that sends toxins into the brain. When you push your body beyond its capacities, it produces cortisol that stresses the brain. Memory problems and concentration can result. So get off the couch for the good of your body and your brain, but don't run yourself, or them, into the ground. Consider these approaches instead.

Individual Exercise Methods

Your brain falls into a beneficial rhythm when you perform individual exercises, like dancing or swimming. The cerebellum, the motor ridge in the parietal lobe, and the frontal regions are all affected positively. The cerebellum is that part of the brain at the back under the cortex. It has zillions of nerve connections to the rest of the brain. It is considered the hub for balance and body coordination and it also has key connections to the frontal lobe. There is ample evidence that exercises requiring balance and coordination can ease the symptoms of attention deficit disorder, providing better mental focus.

The theoretical scenario is that higher activity in the cerebellum creates extra nerve connections over the entire body, such as increased coordination and visual-spatial connections, as the needs arise. Suffice it to say that, regardless of what happens, exercise does help these functions.

The areas of the motor ridge (in the center of your brain) and the frontal lobe also coordinate thoughts and executive functions. A gentle workout helps improve thought processes in both senior executives and schoolchildren. There are many exercises that will work. You should pick those that serve your interests and circumstances. Here are some recommended individual exercises for your consideration:

- "Air conducting" an orchestra (you might want to do this out of view of all but your closest friends)

- Slow dancing

- Tai chi

- Yoga

- Swimming laps

- Drumming a consistent pattern on a drum

- Singing

- Playing a musical instrument

- Walking

Team Exercises

Team exercises provide additional benefits by stimulating the brain's problem solving, memory, and reactive coordination. Even a game of poker stimulates your brain dramatically. If it doesn't, I'd like to play Texas hold 'em with you sometime. More physical sports like table tennis or basketball benefit your reactive coordination. And if you win, you get mood elevation too!

The areas of the brain affected include the frontal lobes, the cerebellum, the temporal lobe, the parietal motor regions, and the occipital lobe. The temporal lobe handles social relations, emotional states, and memory, all of which are put to work in these exercises.

The group exercises that come to mind are:

- Volleyball

- Tennis

- Hiking in groups

- Dancing with a partner

- Playing a musical instrument in a band

- Singing with a group

- Table tennis

MENTAL EXERCISE

The old saying that "you have to use it or lose it" holds true for both muscle and mental strength. A muscle atrophies about 3 percent for each day of idleness due to fiber decay. The idle brain loses punch too. It begins to lose the dendrite connections with major centers, and receptor sites fall away, blocking the passage of neuron transmissions. The best way to prevent dementia is to keep exercising the brain with mental challenges. Watching television—except *Dr. Phil,* of course—and playing one-handed solitaire don't qualify as brain exercise.

Just as physical exercise generates strength in various parts of the brain, mental exercise builds strength in the exercised parts of the brain. Individual mental exercises generally affect the three areas of the frontal (executive region), temporal (memory), and occipital lobes (visual imagery).

Mind games for adults aren't limited to the word problems and crosswords in the American Airlines magazine. I have listed some games, including a few from the America Mensa library, for your consideration. Mensa is an organization for those who rank in the top 2 percent of the population intellectually. Its mission is to foster human intelligence. I have been the supervisory psychologist for this fine organization for a number of years. Its members are some of the most gracious people I've met, and, needless to say, they are pretty sharp cookies too. Mensa members love to play mental games to stimulate their minds. Here are some of their favorites:

Games

3 Stones
10 Days in Africa
Abalone
Apples to Apples
Avalam
Basari
Blokus
Bollox
Brainstrain

The Bridges of Shangri-La
Char
Chung Toi
Cityscape
Clue—The Great Museum Caper
Continuo
Cube Checkers
Curses!
DAO
Doubles Wild
Down Fall
Duo
Dvonn
Farook
Finish Lines
Fire & Ice
Fluxx
The Great Dalmuti

Puzzles

Mensa Think Smart—Abbie Salny, Ph.D.
Mensa Quiz a Day—Abbie Salny, Ph.D., et al.
Mensa Book of Words—Abbie Salny, Ph.D.
Mensa Genius ABC Quiz Book—Alan Stillson
Great Word Search Puzzles for Kids—Mark Danan

Interpersonal Games

Bridge
Chess
Checkers
Poker
Bingo
Charades
Clue

A MAJOR LIFESTYLE DIRECTION: CHEWING

Here is a recommendation guaranteed to drive teachers up the wall: One of the most valuable behaviors a child or adult can do to clear a foggy brain is to chew. This is especially true if the substance you are chewing contains *xylitol*. I know that may seem hard to swallow (sorry), so let me explain why and how it works.

If you ordinarily breathe through your mouth, you lose IQ points. We've found this to be true for Alzheimer's victims and patients with a variety of mental disorders, such as ADHD, OCD, and even mental retardation. Even people who breathe through their mouths when sleeping have less oxygen flowing to their brains and hearts, making them more prone to cardiovascular problems like heart attacks and strokes.

The reason seems to relate to the nasal cavities' closer proximity to the brain. So, when you breathe in through your nose, you get a natural infusion of nitric oxide, a very powerful gas that helps your brain and body process air more effectively. It supercharges your neurological system. By breathing through your nose, you absorb more oxygen and cleaner air.

Interestingly, breast-feeding appears to teach children to develop this more effective breathing process. That lesson may well be more important to his or her brain than the natural nutritional elements derived from breast milk. One of the reasons chewing can be helpful for breathing is that the action of the jaws helps open up your nasal passages. It also promotes better jaw development, which in turn creates bigger nasal passages. Some scientists believe that moving your jaw joints decreases anxiety and focuses your mind. That is one of the reasons ADHD kids move their joints so much when attempting to focus.

Chewing also helps prevent tooth decay. Cavities and loss of teeth are detriments to mental alertness. When older people lose their teeth, especially their molars, their nasal passages also close down. This causes them to breathe through their mouths.

I'm going to clue you in on a little something to chew on. Xylitol is a sugar substitute that tastes good, *very* good. And the best news is that it is good for you too (hard to believe, I know). Xylitol prevents cavities, develops better teeth, and does a great job of encouraging you to breathe through your nose. I don't own any xylitol processing plants, but I love to give these gum products to my ADHD kids. They think it's a treat and it really helps them mentally and physically. It also helps older adults, as it prevents tooth decay and encourages better breathing.

There are many products with xylitol that are available on the Internet.

SOME FINAL THOUGHTS

We've looked at lifestyle factors that affect your brain, either positively or negatively. The good news is that you can change your lifestyle and improve your brainpower with just a few minor adjustments. You can make your environment more stimulating by developing new habits that exercise your body and your mind. Both your brain and your body need to be nurtured. Exercising them has great benefits even if they've been neglected for a while. Your body and brain have incredible restorative powers. Regeneration is a marvel of the body, but poor habits can impede that great power. The next chapter gives you methods for restoring that gift.

Six

RESTORING YOUR BRAINPOWER

SLEEP FACTS AND STATS

- Before Thomas Edison's invention of the lightbulb, people slept an average of 10 hours a night; today Americans average 6.9 hours of sleep on weeknights and 7.5 hours per night on weekends (National Sleep Foundation, 2002 Sleep in America poll).

- Sleep deprivation and sleep disorders are estimated to cost Americans over $100 billion annually in lost productivity, medical expenses, sick leave, and property and environmental damage (National Sleep Foundation).

- More than two-thirds of all children (69 percent) experience one or more sleep problems at least a few nights a week (2004 Sleep in America poll).

- While many Americans enjoy the benefits of sufficient sleep, as many as 47 million adults may be putting themselves at risk for injury, health, and behavior problems because they aren't meeting their minimum sleep need in order to be fully alert the next day (2002 Sleep in America poll).

- Up to 40 percent of adults report at least occasional difficulty sleeping; chronic and/or severe insomnia affects about 10 to 15 percent of adults, according to the National Institutes of Health (NIH). Direct costs of insomnia, which include dollars spent on insomnia treatment, health care services, hospital care, and nursing home care, are estimated at nearly $14 billion annually. Indirect costs such as work loss, property damage from accidents, and transportation to and from health care providers are estimated to be $28 billion.

- The National Highway Traffic Safety Administration conservatively estimates that drowsy drivers cause 100,000 police-reported crashes each year. (That is about 1.5 percent of all crashes.) These crashes result in more than 1,500 fatalities and 71,000 injuries and cost an estimated $12.5 billion in diminished productivity and property loss.

- According to the National Sleep Foundation's 2002 Sleep in America poll, 51 percent of Americans said they drove while feeling drowsy in the past year; 17 percent said they actually dozed off behind the wheel.

Here's a very easy pop quiz. You might even call it a "no brainer."

What's the most common reason that people don't perform up to their intellectual potential?

And the answer is . . . lack of sleep!

Didn't catch you napping on that one, did I?

I wouldn't be surprised if I did. Insomnia is one of the greatest health problems today. A majority (51 to 75 percent) of the population complains of sleep deprivation or insomnia. For most of those who say they don't sleep well, the problem is chronic, not acute.

Chronic lack of sleep has a huge impact on the brain. It can trigger depression, anxiety, alcohol and drug abuse, difficulties in concentration, and loss of endurance in cognitive processing (also known as "the attention span of a hummingbird"). The physical toll from sleep deprivation is staggering. It can cause cardiovascular, pulmonary, and gastrointestinal disorders. Many people say they don't sleep enough because they have so much work to do. But the sad truth is that poor sleeping habits create an economic burden on society in lost productivity and health care costs.

Pills and alcohol are the enemies of restful sleep. They produce an unhealthy sleep that is neither restorative nor conducive to your natural cycles. They have a high rebound effect, which means that withdrawing from the drug can cause even more sleeplessness, and can be highly addictive psychologically as well as physically. Lack of sleep is a major problem in society, yet few treatment centers devote resources to this is-sue. PsyMed, a consulting firm devoted to the diagnosis and treatment of sleep disorders, partners with Texas Medical in offering the only major treatment program available. It is an anti-insomnia program I created called "Rhythms of Sleep."

There is a dramatic difference in performance levels between a fatigued brain and one that is rested and fully functioning. If you started with an IQ score of 100, which is average, and went three days without restorative sleep, your brain would function only in the IQ range of 75, which is the borderline learning range (common to writers and parents of teenagers).

It's scary to think about doctors and nurses who work long hours without sleep and then have to make life-or-death decisions in split sec-onds. It's just as alarming to consider that a truck driver operating a forty-ton semitrailer truck at seventy miles per hour may be roaring up on your car with very little sleep to keep his mind alert.

THE UNDERLYING ASSESSMENT OF QUALITY OF SLEEP

Sleep is not something that works with the flip of a switch. It is a dynamic process in which you flow from one stage to another. There are five stages of sleep commonly thought to be essential for a good body and brain re-charge.

- Stage 1: This is the "fall" in falling asleep. It is a transition stage between wakefulness and sleep. It usually lasts between one and five minutes and occupies approximately 2 to 5 percent of a normal night of sleep. This stage is dramatically increased in some insomnia, restless leg disorders, and sleep-interferers such as apnea and alcohol usage before sleep.

- Stage 2: This is the "baseline" of sleep. It is part of the ninety-minute cycle and occupies approximately 45 to 60 percent of total sleep time.

- Stages 3 and 4, or Delta sleep: In stages 3 and 4, sleep evolves into Delta sleep or "slow wave" sleep in approximately ten to twenty minutes and may last fifteen to thirty minutes. It is called "slow wave" sleep because brain activity slows down dramatically from the Theta rhythm of Stage 2 to a much slower rhythm of one to two cycles per second called Delta and the height or amplitude of the waves increases dramatically. In most adults these two stages are completed within the first two ninety-minute sleep cycles or within the first three hours of sleep. Contrary to popular belief, it is Delta sleep that is the "deepest" stage of sleep (not REM) and the most restorative. It is Delta sleep that a sleep-deprived person's brain craves first and foremost. In children, Delta sleep can occupy up to 40 percent of all sleep time, and this is what makes children nearly "dead asleep" and impossible to awaken during most of the night. Adults often express extreme envy over this ability to "sleep like a baby."

- Stage 5, REM (rapid eye movement sleep): This is a very active stage of sleep. It consumes 20 to 25 percent of a normal night's sleep. Breathing, heart rate, and brain wave activity quicken. Vivid dreams can occur. Sleep specialists call this fifth stage of sleep REM, or rapid eye movement, sleep because our eyes tend to move rapidly about. After REM stage, the body usually returns to Stage 2 sleep.

CONSEQUENCES OF POOR SLEEP PATTERNS

If you just miss a few hours of sleep now and then, your body can compensate. But if you consistently miss out on hours of sleep you will likely end up being one sick *and* tired puppy. Should you miss REM sleep for ten days or more, depression and agitation will dog your weary soul. That much lost sleep will surely hurt your performance on the job and guarantee that you won't be much fun to hang out with.

You need your Stage 1 and 2 sleep to function at a normal level. If you don't get it, stress will mess with every aspect of your life. You will probably even gain weight as fat accumulates due to ongoing adrenal output. Sleep Stages 3 and 4 are very important for physical restoration. You'll be

According to Morin, Colecchi, Stone, Sood, & Brink, who concluded after conducting a peer-reviewed study comparing medication and behavioral approaches to insomnia (*Journal of the American Medical Association* 281 [2002], 991–999), behavioral approaches were as good as, if not better than, medication.

less tolerant of pain related to fibromyalgia and myofascial pain syndrome. There is a strong correlation between lack of sleep and back and neck pain, not to mention diabetes, arthritis, and lupus. More bad news for sleepless souls: your immune system needs more than forty winks to keep its guard up, so when you go without adequate sleep, you are more vulnerable to viral infections.

WHAT TO DO

So, you get the message: No snooze? You lose! We've got to get you back into the serious Z's so that you can perform at an A-level. The good news is that there are ways to restore your quality sack time so that your brain gets enough time to recharge. Here are three proven approaches that involve modifying your circadian rhythms, lowering stress levels, and, finally, one strategy that sounds delightfully bovine: rumination control.

CIRCADIAN RHYTHMS

Your biological clock is set to the "circadian rhythm." This is the cycle we instinctively follow for optimum mental and physical health. Each of us has a unique set of circadian rhythms, and if we disrupt them we suffer the results in the form of fatigue, pain, stress, and even death.

The January 2005 Issue of *Pediatrics* shows that teenagers whose school schedules start at 7:30 a.m. cannot regain their circadian rhythms and remain sleepy most of the day.

Anyone who has traveled across several time zones by plane has experienced jet lag—that groggy realization that while your day is beginning in Washington, D.C., the night you just left in San Francisco is hardly over. Jet lag is a reminder that your body is set to a twenty-four-hour clock. Hence the Latin phrase *circa dies,* meaning "about one day," becomes *circadian rhythm.* This internal biological clock is what makes all organisms tick. Even ticks. It influences the release of hormones that play a role in sleep and wakefulness, metabolic rate, and body temperature.

Most of us who are not teenagers, jazz musicians, or characters in an Anne Rice novel are tuned to a circadian rhythm that calls for sleep and restoration when the sun is on the other side of our earth. This is also known as nighttime, the right time. Our brains and bodies are ready to rock approximately a half day (twelve hours) after we've had our deepest sleep. If we adjusted our schedules to perform our most demanding tasks during that peak time, we'd be primed for four hours on each side of noon. This would be just dandy except that work often gets in the way of sleep.

When the demands of work disrupt our sleep rhythms, our natural restorative processes begin to shut down. Shift workers are enormously affected by their unnatural hours, especially if they cannot establish a stable pattern. These shifts can also pertain to lifestyle patterns as well (staying out too late, watching TV into the morning hours, drinking alcohol excessively, etc.).

Alcohol and sugar affect our sleep cycles. So does staying up half the night sending IM messages to your friends. Or playing video games until the owls stop hooting. You must take responsibility for your own safe and restful sleep. If you aren't getting enough, then it's up to you to make a change to get back on track in the sack. Health is a choice. By taking responsibility, you can take control, and you will reap the benefits.

TAKING CHARGE OF OUR CIRCADIAN RHYTHMS

Sleeping rituals:

Consider the preliminary steps to sleep as a ritual. Rituals are important because they send messages to our bodies about what is expected to happen. Most important, they help synchronize circadian rhythms. What are your rituals for preparing for a peak performance? For bedtime? (Turning out the lights, television, prayers, etc.) Have you ever found it almost impossible to wake up and start your day, especially after a difficult time going to sleep? Your brain is still asleep. You are literally sleepwalking, and maybe sleep-talking too! You've got to wake up your brain with stimulation, and I'm not talking Starbucks. This is where you can put into practice some of the things you've already learned in this book. BAUD, music, and physical exercises will get your brain up and running.

If you want to calm the brain to invite restful sleep, it's time for soft, slow music, relaxed muscles, low lighting, and a secure situation. The environmental factors listed below may need to be adjusted to soothe you.

✓ Noise
✓ Light
✓ Comfort
✓ Safety (locking the doors, checking the house, etc.)

Ritual behavior for enhancing the active period:

_____   _____

_____   _____

_____   _____

Rituals for enhancing the sleep or restoration period:

_____   _____

_____   _____

_____   _____

Awareness:

The first step is to become aware of your rhythm. Identify the times of day you feel most effective and useful consistently. Note the kinds of things you like to do. Also note your least active and least focused periods, and what you like to do. (This may be when you are normally sleeping or trying to sleep, so this might not be the best estimation.)

6:00–8:00 A.M._____

8:00–10:00 A.M._____

10:00 A.M.–noon_____

noon–2:00 P.M._____

2:00–4:00 P.M._____

4:00–6:00 P.M._____

6:00–8:00 P.M._____

8:00–10:00 P.M._____

10:00 P.M.–midnight_____

midnight–2:00 A.M._____

2:00–4:00 A.M._____

4:00–6:00 A.M._____

Acknowledge Needed Changes

Make a note of the kinds of activities you do in order to modify your circadian rhythm to meet your requirements, such as drinking coffee or taking stimulants, drinking alcohol, taking sedatives, exercising, eating food, etc. Indicate how well these work for this purpose. Also note what kinds of activities might be explored (nutrition, relaxation, etc.).

LEARNING TO DE-STRESS YOUR SLEEP

It's no surprise that stress is a major hindrance to effective sleep. When a person experiences stress, a biochemical reaction occurs in the brain. It's an alert system: the old fight-or-flight alarm that has kept our species around despite the fact that we weren't exactly the biggest or baddest creatures around, even after the extinction of the saber-toothed tiger. Stress is actually a good thing for human survival, but a bad thing for sleep. When you are stressed, your hormones are alerted to call to action your body's emergency response system—which means a higher heart rate, higher muscle tension, more adrenaline flow for energy, and a host of other reactions diametrically opposed to a sleep state. None of these is exactly conducive to nappy time.

Ninety percent of the population admits to at least one episode in which stress has kept them awake at night. But what do they do about it, other than complain? Taking medication doesn't work over the long term because drugs only dull the symptoms. They don't address the source of the anxiety or depression that's keeping you up.

Probably the easiest thing you can do to induce a restful sleep is to listen to music designed specifically for that purpose. I recommend the CDs at Mindbodyseries.com. This is a good and simple option. Otherwise, you might waste a lot of time stressing out about stress, which doesn't allow for much sleep. This mental activity just spins your brain into high beta, which means "low sleep." Listen to the sleep CD and follow the steps until your body and brain go with the flow. The CD literally teaches your brain how to go to sleep. It's elevator music, with a benevolent purpose.

FOLLOW A SCRIPT

There are several scripts I recommend for helping you sleep. One script is listed in the appendix of this book and is for general release of stress. The general release program will train you to focus on the breathing patterns necessary for sleep. Breathing cycles take on a slower and more balanced inhalation/exhalation pattern during restful sleep. If a person breathes too fast or too slowly, the body will react to inhibit sleep. If you breathe too fast, that is a signal to the rest of the body to become alert and deal with a problem. If you breathe too slowly, your brain will become anxious because it is not getting enough oxygen.

As you have already learned, you can control your breathing patterns, and in doing so can learn to vastly diminish the effects of stress on your body and mind. If you are breathing in a non-sleep-conducive pattern, your brain will invent stress to be consistent with your balance. Take a moment and intentionally breathe out more than you breathe in, or vice versa, and see what happens to your stress level.

The breathing approach is basically a method for learning to breathe in and out in the same levels. Perhaps the easiest approach is to count the seconds of each out-breath and each in-breath. Take a breath in, and slowly release it so it is out by the time you count to seven. If it helps, you might want to repeat a positive phrase instead of the numbers, such as "I am getting more and more relaxed," or "I am feeling more at peace with God," or "I am strong and perfect."

RUMINATION CONTROL

The mind goes through a series of processes before it creates emotional responses. This is called the A-B-C pattern. The first step in the beginning of emotional response begins with the image (step A) of historical, future, or current event. You cannot respond to something unless you identify it. You cannot become afraid of a snake if you are not aware of its presence, for example.

A   Awareness of something to respond to
B   Recognizing meaningfulness to the object or event
C   Responding with the associated learned response

The second step is to recognize the event or object. This usually comes from an associated memory that puts things in context. If you have never seen a snake, never been educated as to the dangers of a snake, never experienced any context with a snake, you could not have an emotional response since there would not be a context of recognition.

The third phase is to respond with a learned or expected emotional response. If your meaningful context is one of fear, you would likely have an emotional response typical of your other fearful responses. However, we all have our unique library of emotional responses based on the expected consequences (protection, support, etc.).

In the earlier section on controlling your circadian rhythms, I discussed preparing your sleep environment by becoming aware of noise disturbances, but the most frequent "noise" affecting sleep patterns is the noise coming from your own mind. That noise is often the screeching of your mind trying to integrate your worries into some workable solution with pieces that don't fit. It is as if you are trying to find peace and a sense of stability without a coherent plan.

Let me explain a phenomenon of the mind that is very relevant to sleep and restoration. The mind is a problem solver. That is its function. Your mind keeps churning when you go to bed because it is searching for some meaning in the chaos of the information you've dumped into it all day. Have you ever watched a dog in a deep sleep on the floor? Well, a dog can sleep like that because its mind isn't trying to figure out how to cut $10,000 off the Visa bill by the end of the month while still making the house payment!

Don't envy the dog its deep sleep. Learn how to sleep like a dog instead of working like one.

SIMPLIFY YOUR BRAIN AND REACH THE PEACEFUL STEPS INTO SLEEP

Step One:

The first step is to stop ruminating about problems, real or imagined. When we continue to focus our thoughts at night on information that is unusable and unsolvable we only waste energy and efforts, making ourselves more restless and agitated. Imagine a wastebasket. Now imagine throwing those disruptive thoughts in the wastebasket. It can be that easy.

Rehashing Troublesome Events

It is a waste of time to try to figure out why people did or did not do something. You cannot change what has already happened. You cannot make things happen differently. And beating yourself up forever won't help you live your life. Yes, we all do things we wish we had not done. And we will always wonder if things might have come out differently if we had studied or played harder. You will never find simplified answers in this pile of data, so eliminate those issues now.

Future Fears Aren't Worth the Funk

We have all awakened in the middle of the night because our minds have been trying to decide a course of action for solving a pending problem. It would be nice if our bodies could just go ahead and sleep, but it doesn't work that way. When the mind is working, the body responds by pumping blood to the brain and the organs. So you've got to shut it all down by switching your mind off or giving it a far more relaxing task.

Stirring the Pot of Anger

It is easy to fall into a pattern of playing out a bad scene over and over again in your mind. But in most cases, this only serves to cause more and more anxiety. I once treated a patient who couldn't stop replaying a scene in which he asked for a raise and his boss turned him down. He was upset for a month with this recurring thought, and finally one day he went in and quit. His boss was actually going to give him a raise eventually but did not get the opportunity. Result: Loss of sleep, loss of rational thinking, and loss of money.

Making Sleep a Competitive Goal

Too often individuals who have trouble with sleep begin to think about this problem as a failure in performing some competitive task. I have heard people say, "I will be facing another failure tonight." So they make two mistakes: They begin to program themselves all day for failure to sleep, and they try too hard at the art of sleeping. Sleeping is the art of letting go of competition and demand, not an act of rigid self-determination. That defeats the process.

Sleep is not a competition. Nobody is grading you. Nobody is scoring you. So stop playing games with your sleep.

Step Two:

Put your mind in neutral. Shut off the thinking that is driving sleep from your mind. Make it a habit to relax your mind and then your body. Here are three methods for doing that.

1. Method One

Use a "sleep" CD. Just listening to the instructions takes your mind off worrisome things and introduces you to a better state of mind. You don't have to figure out problems or maintain focus or eliminate thoughts. All you have to do is follow the directions.

2. Method Two

Focus on the present process, eliminating thoughts about the past or future. If you become aware of drifting into these no-no areas, immediately stop those thought patterns and resume present thoughts. Focus on your breathing. That will bring you into the present. Feel each breath and its effect on your body. Feel the air enter your lungs and leave through your nose. Place all your attention on your breath and put everything else out of your mind. This takes some discipline, so don't beat yourself up if your mind wanders.

3. Method Three

Select music that you enjoy, preferably something that has no melody but repeats soothing patterns of sound. New Age music works for some. I prefer Native American flute music. I wouldn't recommend Yoko Ono, but that's just me. I'd also stay away from inspirational songs that make you want to solve world problems, or those country western sob songs that make you want to drive your pickup truck in front of a train in the rain. Listed below are some recommendations for music selections for your interest.

Lullaby: A Collection (Various Artists)	Music for Little People
John Serrie, *Lumia Nights*	Neuronion Records
John Serrie, *Spirit Keepers*	New World Music, Inc.
Wind Riders, *Wind Riders*	Talking Taco Music, Inc.
Debbie Danbrook, *Miracles*	Healing Music
Johannes Linstead, *Guitarra del Fuego*	Real Music

A WORD OF INTEREST

Sleep is one of the greatest joys of your life, and as you get older, it gets to be even more important, and more difficult to enjoy. It is the time for physical restoration and mental recharging. I like to think of it as the time when angels dance in your head. If you believe that you have a soul, you must also know that it is immortal. To maintain it within the confines of a body and to batter it with the demands of a daily life is to confine it. Set your spirit free. Sleep is intended to be joyful as well as restorative. It is not a demand for performance or an expectation we place on ourselves.

There is no reason to feel guilty or irresponsible if you have had difficulty sleeping. A lot of factors can disrupt normal sleeping patterns. Sleep can be inconsistent because of the earth's gravity or the shift in the weather. It can be as elusive as a lover at times. But as with all true blessings, once it comes to you, the rewards are like a kiss on your heart.

Seven

THE SIX FACES OF GENIUS

At twenty-seven, Jason was a rising star in the law firm he joined after earning his degree with honors. He was athletic, smart, popular, and from a wealthy family. Despite the aura of success and accomplishment that surrounded him, Jason was having trouble deciding who he was and what role he wanted to take in the world.

Jason was the son of a powerful and influential man, a national leader. He had grown up hiding in the shadow of his father. But when it came time to step out of that shadow and forge his own identity, he struggled. Jason had always looked to his father for approval and validation. As he entered manhood, he had trouble approving and validating himself. Like his father, Jason projected a swaggering, even bullying self-confidence. But when I spoke with him, I perceived a frightened kid whose self-esteem was riddled with doubt, especially in those situations unreachable by the family influence. Inside the circles where his family ties were known, Jason played his father's son, projecting the same strong personality traits as his powerful father. But in situations where no one knew his family connections, Jason became timid and withdrawn.

Jason had reached the point where his life was in his own hands. He'd arrived there a bit later than most because he'd gone straight from his undergraduate degree to law school. So for the first time, he had to step outside the very comfortable role of his father's son. Jason didn't like the pressure. He wasn't sure who he was besides the son of a famous man. He had few true friends and even his "babe" girlfriend seemed to be more attracted to his family's status than to him as a person. It was no wonder, then, that Jason found himself depressed and a bit lost several months after graduation.

He'd landed in a top law firm in part because of his performance in law school but also, to a great degree, because of his father's powerful position and influence. But his law partners expected Jason to perform at the highest levels in order to justify his salary. He was scared. He felt isolated. And he didn't know who to turn to because he didn't want to be perceived as weak or needy. Instead of bucking up and proving his value as a lawyer, he dropped out. Jason announced that his real love was writing and that he intended to pursue it as a career.

He failed to understand that people only read the works of authors who have something valuable, or at least entertaining, to impart. Jason was not a particularly introspective or wise young man, and he lacked the experience to compensate. He realized this and used it to "hide out" by moving from job to job, claiming that he was building up a wide range of experience to tap into in his writings. It was a clever strategy because it allowed him to postpone any real goals. It also reduced expectations from others. But it did nothing to boost Jason's self-confidence. He knew that he was scamming everyone.

While in search of experience, Jason journeyed to South America. There, he witnessed shamanic healing rituals that fascinated him with their primitive dances and guttural intonations. Through a guide and interpreter who accompanied him, the young man asked the shaman about his method, only to have the jungle healer look directly into his eyes and respond with a question of his own:

"You have come to know who you really are, haven't you?"

Jason was startled and initially defensive but found himself drawn to the shaman.

"What can you tell me of my destiny? What can you tell me of what I am to be?" he asked.

The shaman offered a smile marked by broken and missing teeth. He motioned for Jason to sit with him, and they talked for hours that day. The shaman smoked a pipe of unknown ingredients and listened. Finally, he said: "Young man, I knew you were coming from the spirits, and they tell me you are strong. You have a strange and precarious life ahead of you because others have lived your life for you, depriving you of knowing who you are. Consequently you only know one part of yourself, the bull."

Jason struggled to understand: "What do you mean, my 'bull'?"

"People have many facets, much like jewels," the shaman responded. "When we know only one part, we limit our opportunities and our knowledge of ourselves. You are a bull because that is the calling and pleasure of your father, but you are much more. Your father is also much more, but he is no concern to me. You are much more, like a jewel."

The shaman let Jason ponder that for nearly an hour, refusing to answer any further questions while he smoked the pipe in silence. Finally, the shaman began to speak again. Jason thought he was being clever by covertly operating a tape recorder. Later, he'd find that the tape was blank.

"We are all one soul with many faces. You grow stronger when you know these faces and wear them wisely. Our ceremonial masks represent our many faces. You have been wearing your mask of the bull, which is a strong mask, but you cannot only be a bull and live wisely." The shaman laughed. "You can be a bull with your girlfriends, but never with your mother or wife."

He pointed to Jason's chest and said, "You must become your wolf, and then your beaver, before you become who you want to be."

Jason was puzzled, but restrained himself from questioning further when the shaman raised his hand to silence him. He could tell that the shaman was tired, but he hoped that he could understand more before he was dismissed. He was disappointed when the shaman slowly arose and walked away to his hut.

Jason's interpreter said, "He has done what he is going to do. You are now supposed to give him a gift for his wisdom."

Jason reached into his pocket for some money as he asked, "How much?"

The interpreter explained, "He does not want money. He doesn't buy things anyway. But he does like American cigarettes and beer."

As Jason rode back to his hotel, he pondered the shaman's words. "Our culture teaches us that we have one soul that lives forever, but the shaman spoke of at least six faces or masks that we show to the world," he reflected.

His interpreter told him that the six basic masks were: the wolf, the eagle, the snake, the bull, the deer, and the beaver.

Jason whispered, "And I am a bull?"

The interpreter quickly explained, "You are using your mask as a bull, most of the time. The shaman explained that you use this too much."

Jason asked, "What does this mean?"

The interpreter smiled because he was in training to become a shaman, and he was pleased that he had an audience to practice his knowledge. "The wolf is the teacher within us who we become in order to carry on our traditions. The eagle has keen eyes that see above the horizon. We become eagles to see beyond ourselves. The snake is mysterious and its venom carries healing powers. The bull, which you overuse, is the powerful warrior with very narrow but intense vision. The deer is the giver and nurturer, and the beaver is the builder of our world. He has vision for details and constructive power."

Jason was stunned. "You mean that I must learn these other parts of myself. As a bull, or warrior, I have focused too much on bullying my way into things. Which mask should I begin to use now?"

The interpreter shrugged his shoulders. "What is your challenge? The mask matches the challenge."

Jason thought for several minutes, trying to isolate his problems. "I guess it would be friendship first. I think I compete with everyone and I don't trust anyone, really."

"So you want to *build* relationships and friends," said the interpreter, with an emphasis on the word "build." He wanted Jason to get the idea without making it too easy or simplistic.

Jason got it immediately. "I must become a beaver. How do I do that? Wear a beaver mask?"

"You Americans are so literal. You must learn how to be a team member, to begin to trust others toward a mutual goal. You must become sensitive to their tasks and personal abilities. This mask is not a disguise; it is part of yourself and a set of skills. If you want to build relationships, you have to know what this requires. You have not had a model in your life for this, have you?"

Jason looked sad. "I have spent all my life learning to be a bull, I guess."

The interpreter responded with a giggle, "And you have learned it well, very well. Don't sacrifice it for another. It will come in handy. You are not a bad person for overusing it, just not in balance."

The end of this story has yet to be played out, but Jason did learn the "beaver" ways. He gained friends as a result, and he gained wisdom too. Eventually, he returned to the practice of law where his mastery of other masks made him a formidable force in criminal trials.

FACETS OF SELF AND SCIENCE

Integrity and balance are the keys to personal strength. Our lives have many facets. We are a bundle of traits and contradictions. Think of a thick rope made of many individual strands. When integrated and wound together carefully, those single strands have a power far greater than they would individually. Our challenge is to integrate the many aspects of who we are into the most powerful single entity we can become. "United we stand, divided we fall."

That was the basis of the shaman's lesson for Jason. Our power lies in integrating the many facets of our personalities. The same message is found in the work of early pioneers in psychology, such as William James and Carl Jung. And there is a biological basis within the brain that explains our multiple personality attributes or "facets of the jewel." These multiple neural capacities may well be required for survival.

Brendan O'Regan and Caryle Hirshberg conducted a mammoth research project on spontaneous cancer remissions in people who did not seek medical treatment. They found two consistent traits in these survivors:

1. Each patient was determined to make a life change.

2. Each made a transformational personality shift.

These patients generally triggered these personality transformations by placing themselves in new and unfamiliar environments that challenged them to make changes in order to survive. A New York woman with lung cancer went to the desert where she underwent a spiritual transformation that helped her shed a self-centered existence, and with it, her cancer.

There are hundreds of reports of people who overcome disease by reorienting their personalities and changing their approaches to life. Near-death experiences (NDE) have been shown to shift certain brain functions and cause personality adjustments. Whether described as a "rebirth" or "spiritual emergence," such transformations have been shown to cause brain reformation shifts that validate the personal experience and biological changes.

The concept of multilevel consciousness was professionally defined as early as 1889, when Pierre Janet postulated that every person has at least two sides to their personality. In 1907, Morton Prince suggested that the term *subconscious* might be understood as the simultaneous activity of two or more systems of awareness in one individual. More recently, John Beahrs theorized that we should look upon the sum total of a person's consciousness as the personality.

Carl Jung described the features of multiple consciousnesses as "complexes or splinter psyches." Using word association tests, he concluded that the ego is the center for subpersonalities that protect the central self with different kinds of strengths and powers. He identified the *shadow,* the *anima* (male) and *animus* (female), the archetype of the *spirit* and the *self.*

All of the pioneers in psychology endorsed the existence of—and the need for—multiple types of conscious selves. The brain structure is designed to allow for combined and possibly independent contributors to these personality factors. Normal consciousness is believed to have its origin in the "triune brain," a theoretical organization of three mentalities apparently evolving out of the instincts of survival. The oldest component, the *reptilian brain,* includes the brain stem and much of the reticular system. These components are the basic essentials for life and are therefore associated with the most primitive of animals such as snakes, turtles, and alligators. These reptiles have no pleasure centers and none of the characteristics we usually appreciate as being truly "human." Not to disrespect reptiles, but I can think of a few people who more closely resemble snakes, turtles and alligtors in many regards.

The brain's second level, the *paleomammalian brain,* includes the limbic system and midbrain. This is the emotional component that houses pleasure and social centers. This is the area from which we draw the ability to form communities for survival and comfort. The third level, the *neomammalian brain,* or *neocortex,* includes the remainder of the brain's "computer" components. It is the seat for intellectual machinations, including learning and calculation.

Freud proposed that the psyche was divided into three coexisting parts: the id, the ego, and the superego. While the ego serves both the id (reptilian brain) and the superego (emotional or limbic brain), the conscious strategies for survival and success depend on healthy neurological functioning of all three centers for maximum strength. If the id impulses are weak, your mental energy will lag.

The defining component of human consciousness, the basic brain fixture, takes the form of a bridge of fibers between the left and right brains called the *corpus callosum*. It allows us the luxury—or the agony—of self-reflection. When you stand between two mirrors you can see both sides of yourself. Thanks to the corpus callosum, the two sides of the brain can be coordinated to allow you to reflect internally on your actions and experiences.

We can get "stuck" within one aspect of our personalities when we refuse to reflect on our "whole" selves. A negative self-image of victimization is just such a trap. There is a certain amount of security in adopting this role but it is a self-defeating concept. It is this self-confinement into specific personality labels that restricts our potential. Jason identified with his father's "bull" persona so much that this was all he knew or wanted to know. Please note that this is not a matter of "multiple or split personalities." Multiple personality disorders, which are overhyped, are the result of an anxiety disorder in which a person dissociates under high stress. It is an escape mechanism, a form of self-protection in which distinct personalities form as a place of refuge.

"Split personality" is another term for schizophrenia, or a dysfunction within one personality. A schizophrenic might cry and laugh at the same time. The connections within the individual's reality are simply dysfunctional.

ASSESSING YOUR POWER SELVES

There are many models for varied personality types within individuals, but let's adopt the shaman's version of six types for simplicity's sake. We are going to assess how his model applies to you.

Answer each of the following statements as to whether they are descriptive of your strengths and abilities (D), they are partially descriptive

(PD), they are descriptive of how you would like to be but you feel you lack the abilities (LD), you are rarely aware of such a description of yourself (RD), or they are not desired or never considered (ND). Remember that you may use different strengths for different situations or they may vary depending on how stressed you become, so some dimensions may be used more or less frequently than others.

SECTION W (WOLF):

1. I have the ability and patience to teach others truths of life.

   D   PD   LD   RD   ND

2. I appreciate the truths we learn from history.

   D   PD   LD   RD   ND

3. I am sensitive to others and my mission is to help them be the best they can be.

   D   PD   LD   RD   ND

4. I live the life of a teacher and a molder of lives.

   D   PD   LD   RD   ND

5. I believe that the path to satisfaction is in always being a student of life.

   D   PD   LD   RD   ND

SECTION E (EAGLE):

6. I think that I can rise above conflicts and gain perspective on why they exist and their real lessons for me.

   D   PD   LD   RD   ND

7. Life is not as complicated as it seems.

   D   PD   LD   RD   ND

8. I can often see many different sides to an issue, and most of the time I can see both humor and tragedy in all conflict.

   D   PD   LD   RD   ND

9. When assessing a situation, I like to get the big picture instead of focusing on the details.

   D   PD   LD   RD   ND

10. I believe that some problems have no solutions, and that the only way to deal with them is to transcend them and/or to allow time to resolve them.

    D   PD   LD   RD   ND

SECTION S (SNAKE):

11. I see things in other people that they don't see in themselves and I feel compelled to help them in spite of themselves.

    D   PD   LD   RD   ND

12. I perceive what people need for healing, and often ignore their defenses and resistance in order to help them achieve inner health.

    D   PD   LD   RD   ND

13. I depend on my intuition about others to know how to help them.

    D   PD   LD   RD   ND

14. I often do not tell people everything I know about them because I have my own plan for helping them through pain they are not aware of themselves.

    D   PD   LD   RD   ND

15. When I listen to others, I am listening to their whole bodies, including their emotional tones, their body postures, and the underlying stories of their lives as well as to the verbal content they are telling me.

    D   PD   LD   RD   ND

SECTION B (BULL):

16. When I have a goal, I concentrate totally on achieving that goal, ignoring criticisms from others.

    D   PD   LD   RD   ND

17. I know how to use power, and I will for the sake of achieving my objectives.

    D   PD   LD   RD   ND

18. I am often seen as very driven because I pay little attention to others when I set my sights on a purpose.

    D   PD   LD   RD   ND

19. I am often a leader because I know how to achieve the team's objective.

    D   PD   LD   RD   ND

20. I feel that I can achieve whatever goals I aspire to.

    D   PD   LD   RD   ND

SECTION D (DEER):

21. I feel best when I nurture others.

D   PD   LD   RD   ND

22. My mission is to serve others and I do it very well.

D   PD   LD   RD   ND

23. I can participate well in a team, whatever role I am assigned.

D   PD   LD   RD   ND

24. I feel power in seeing others succeed with my help.

D   PD   LD   RD   ND

25. I protect those I care about with all my strength, and when people realize this, they respect me.

D   PD   LD   RD   ND

SECTION BE (BEAVER):

26. I am a detail-oriented person who thoroughly works out the design of an action plan to achieve my goal.

D   PD   LD   RD   ND

27. I think that anything can be achieved with careful planning, and I am very creative in this ability.

D   PD   LD   RD   ND

28. I am very clear in my communications with others.

D   PD   LD   RD   ND

29. I realize the subtle political and psychological tricks it takes to get what I want.

   D   PD   LD   RD   ND

30. I like to develop contracts with others that cover all the details so communication is clear.

   D   PD   LD   RD   ND

Scoring:

For each section, give yourself 4 points for each "D" you circled, 3 points for each PD you circled, 2 points for each LD you circled, and 1 point for each RD you circled. Total the individual items for each section for a range of 5 to 20, and compare them to the general categories below:

Personality State	Very Low	Low	Medium	High	Very High
Section W: Teacher (wolf)	5–6	7–9	10–14	15–18	19–20
Section E: Visionary (Eagle)	5	6–8	9–13	14–18	19–20
Section S: Healer (Snake)	5–6	7–9	10–12	13–18	19–20
Section B: Warrior (Bull)	5	6–8	9–11	13–17	18–20
Section D: Nurturer (Deer)	5	6–9	10–14	15–18	19–20
Section Be: Builder (Beaver)	5–6	7–8	9–12	13–17	18–20

INTERPRETATION OF THE GENIUS SELVES

These six personality states are part of the inherent genius given to you at birth. They are independent of each other. It is possible that you may rank very high on all six. These scales relate to the existence of those states at your disposal for specific situations and emotional states. For example, you may be high in the eagle or visionary state when you are relaxed and in a contemplative mood, but when you get stressed you revert to the beaver (builder) and attend to details.

Using these personality states properly can greatly improve the quality of your life. Your bull personality state may be quite useful in business matters—in fact I have several close friends who are masters of business bull—but the same state may lead to crashes in the china shop of intimate relationships.

The power personality states are positive approaches. But these states are not limited to those noted below. I have eliminated the negative personality states, such as the *victim* or *invisible* states. The victim state relates to a fear-induced approach in which you view yourself as powerless in determining your own fate. The invisible state is one in which you slide behind others in order not to be noticed.

Let's look in greater detail at the basic personality states.

The Wolf (Teacher)

The wolf personality style is that of a teacher. You are the representative of traditions and historically effective lessons. Using your experience as a backdrop for your interactions, you apply your expertise according to the need. You may need to play the role of student from time to time to enhance your teacher powers.

I worked as a clinical professor in the orthopedic surgery division at the Southwestern Medical School under Dr. Vert Mooney, and although Dr. Mooney was a brilliant man, he would often become the student. When I went to him with research ideas, he liked to say, "Treat me like a fourth grader and explain it to me so I might understand." His approach was similar to that of Albert Einstein. While Einstein was serving as a university supervisor, he encountered a student who was struggling to explain his research in quantum physics. Einstein reportedly advised the student: "Slow down so I can follow your ideas."

Both Dr. Mooney and Einstein were brilliant thinkers and teachers. They realized that their influence relied upon both understanding others and being understood. My friend and former student Dr. Phil Mc-Graw was a master of this even before he became famous with his television show. His work at Courtroom Sciences, Inc., in Dallas was masterful. The top lawyers around the country relied on his expertise as a wolf when it came to the psychology of jurors and jury trials.

Dr. Phil's motto for dealing with corporate clients and their lawyers is a great example of the wolf mentality. "You have to know their business better than they do in order to teach them how to win their cases." And he did. He would study engineering, jet engine construction, the fusion rates of subatomic particles, or whatever the client's industry involved before he ever met with them. He became an expert on everything from nicotine biological processing to ozone depletion related to sulfuric exposure. He learned and then he listened. After giving himself a background, he was prepared to understand the subtleties and intricacies of complex legal cases. Once he absorbed the legalities, he would then offer his psychological framework for presenting the case. I've seen him mesmerize top corporate executives and brilliant attorneys with his mastery of their material.

This approach takes time and preparation, not to mention a considerable intellect. If you are in a crisis, you don't have time to steep yourself in vast amounts of information. If a tornado is headed in your direction, you may want to tap into another aspect of your personality.

The Eagle (Visionary)

Most traditional societies attribute sacred powers to the eagle, a majestic, soaring bird. Some have seen it as an intermediary between man and God. The personality state of the eagle empowers you with a bird's-eye view. It gives you the ability to see all sides of a problem. Its greatest asset is the power not simply to resolve a problem, but to rise above and transcend it in the same way that an eagle doesn't cross a mountain, it flies over it. Let's say a teenager is fretting because her boyfriend dumped her. She wallows in excess, even saying she might die of a broken heart. An eagle's view of the same problem would be to rise above and take the wider view. The eagle might envision decades ahead when that former boyfriend turns into a toothless loser who would never have been a worthy partner. The eagle sees that life is a journey of more than a day or two and that today's hurt is often only tomorrow's memory.

The eagle ascends on, rising thermal winds, including those created by laughter and the understanding that you can't take every twist and turn seriously. Sometimes, the joke is on you. Even death and grief can be approached with the philosophy that life itself is a mystery. And that nobody said it was fair. The values we hold while we live are only as good as what we do. Gurus and sages belong to the eagle's nest because of their broad understanding of suffering and joy.

The Snake (Healer)

The snake has long had the mythical reputation as a creature of the underworld, one that travels between the lightness and the darkness of life and death, good and evil. The American Medical Association uses a snake symbol in its insignia. This is a reference to the ancient Greeks' use of yellow snake venom for anesthetizing patients, as it would put them into a deep sleep. Native Americans used rattlesnake venom in their rituals as well.

A person in the snake personality state behaves in mysterious ways, focusing on implicit needs. Just as the shaman mixes potions and salves with some magical knowledge, the snake personality does not reveal the sources of his or her authority. Similar to the lover's power to seduce through intimate knowledge, there is a game of seduction in which the individual reads from a script of power.

My parents taught the snake's personality state to me as I went through school. I was diagnosed as mentally impaired shortly after birth. So my parents wanted to prepare me to meet the world's challenges as best they could. Each year they would sit me down and we would explore my teacher's psychological makeup. One teacher, Ms. Smith, was described to me as a person who was partial to students who put forth great effort. Regardless of how well they performed, if they looked like they were working hard, Ms. Smith always gave them passing grades. My plan was to "look like I was working hard." So every day, regardless of how easy or difficult my assignments were, I would wear this grimace of pain and torment on my face. Actually, I had a pretty easy year, but I carried on the act. When I made good marks, the teacher praised me effusively, and took credit for my amazing performance.

I played the game in college too, analyzing and adjusting my approach to each instructor's style. (It got a little tougher in graduate school, since psychology professors often knew the game better than I did.)

Snake personalities are masters of such games. They are skilled at getting the best performances and results from other people. They can play the healing games so well that people are cured in spite of themselves. They can manage the behavior of the worst children. They can charm the coldest fish in the sea.

The Bull (Warrior)

The bull personality symbolizes the single-minded warrior. This can be a very powerful personality type because there is a sense of purpose and righteousness in a warrior's motivation. Warriors tend not to worry about shades of meaning or collateral damage. Instead, they pursue their goals at any cost. My college roommate was an example of the bull's mentality and discipline. He graduated with honors with a measured IQ of 29. I never saw him write a paper more than one half page with complete sentences. He obviously had learning problems, but his dedication was remarkable.

Individuals suffering from ADHD have difficulty with the bull personality because they cannot concentrate very well, if at all. Unfortunately, this is the personality state that does best in highly structured and regimented environments like the military, sports teams, and Jesuit schools. Parents tend to direct their children into this state because they want them to be focused and success-oriented.

The martial arts are good for developing the bull personality state, which many see as conducive to developing leadership abilities too. It is this model that we hold up in electing our presidents, but then we also want them to be responsive to the needs of a wide array of special interest groups—something that bulls are not particularly good at.

The Deer (Nurturer)

The deer is almost unanimously considered to be the nurturing totem of traditional societies, perhaps because of its gentle nature and its status as the hunter's prime food resource. Most consider the deer to be a symbol of maternal love and physical beauty too. This description is very appropriate to the giving spirit of this personality state. Individuals in this state often use their gentleness for protection as well as power.

Dr. Martin Luther King, Jr., and Gandhi certainly were masters of power through nonviolence. The deer personality appeals to the human conscience.

Dr. King and Gandhi changed the world not by being aggressive, but by being courageously vulnerable. Nelson Mandela, too, proved that standing up for your beliefs without fear of reprisal can disarm even the most determined enemy—especially when the whole world is watching. You have to gauge the situation thoughtfully to know when to play this hand because your enemies may be irrational beyond reach. But many of the greatest events in history were brought about by men and women who adopted the deer personality. (This should be differentiated from the less noble "deer-in-the-headlights" state.)

The Beaver (Builder)

The beaver is a builder of dams. It has remarkable construction and architectural skills. It is also an animal with a limited scope that concentrates on details. This can be a very powerful state for influence. It is my own weakest personality state. I've made enormous efforts to strengthen it.

For several years I worked as a vocational economics expert for the courts in California, New Mexico, and Texas with a firm called, logically enough, Vocational Economics, Inc. My expertise was in calculating lost earning capacities for injured people. There is no small amount of science in applying various statistical government tables, such as survival data and average salaries, to individual cases. If John Q. Case Study suffered a head injury while driving a forklift that was not maintained correctly, the employee might sue the company for negligence. It would be my job to determine the extent of the disability for his head injury, what he might have earned without the head injury, what he was capable of earning with the head injury, and how these figures would predict over his entire work life. It was a numbers game, and my college degree in mathematics and graduate major in statistics served me well with the concepts involved in reaching reasonable predictions. But often the attorneys cross-examining me went after the devil in my details. They raked through my calculations looking for flaws that might destroy my credibility with the jury.

I survived more than twenty-five trials but I was burned by lapses in details on a couple of depositions. For those lapses, I suffered crushing mental anguish. But for the great majority of cases, my practiced focus on details exasperated attorneys trying to discredit me.

THE GENIUS POWER OF THE SIX FACES

Face	Power	Circumstance	Weakness
Wolf	Teaching/ leading	Tradition and using wisdom of the past	Limiting knowledge to the past
Eagle	Vision and future perspective	Offering direction and guidance	Not doing the details
Snake	Insight into motives	Understanding intentions of others	Limiting inspirations
Bull	Focus on goals	Leadership toward objectives	Too narrow a focus, not seeing others
Deer	Nurturing and caring	Giving appreciation and support	Limited objective thinking
Beaver	Coordinating, planning	Group power, mastery over details	Too close to see big picture

As can be seen from the table, there are strengths to each personality. It depends on the situation and the circumstances. There is no perfect face for every situation, unfortunately, so you must be flexible and creative in applying them. The wolf is most powerful in circumstances that call for traditional wisdom and leadership. The eagle's greatest strength lies in rising above and taking the long view. The beaver burrows into the details. The snake sees beyond words and goes to the heart of matters. The deer is a master of gentle influence. The bull charges ahead without fear.

The full integration of these personalities will propel you toward authenticity as you engage the power within you, develop it, and perfect the strengths.

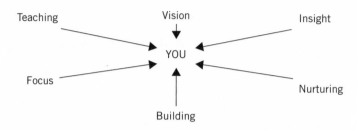

USING THE GENIUS OF THE PERSONALITY FACES

Using the power personality states requires skills and education, as well as shifts in consciousness. You have to identify your weakest states and work to strengthen them. It takes courage, and the awareness that you have no limitations to becoming the person you want to be. You can become a bull, a deer, or any of the other states you choose. You can shift if you decide, but you cannot allow yourself to become trapped into a personality state that no longer serves you.

My role is to teach people to find the appropriate power positions in the face of challenges, even deadly ones. Children are most often in need of refining their personality states because they are the least educated and most controlled by others. I often "coach" them into power states, just as the football coach embraces the warrior state.

Every superstar has a power state. Tony Dorsett of the Dallas Cowboys and Gale Sayers of the Chicago Bears, both former superstars as running backs, once offered their different views of their shared profession.

Tony Dorsett said he saw himself as a tornado, spinning energy off and defeating efforts to tackle him. When a film clip rolled showing him running, indeed he was spinning away from defenders. Gale Sayers offered the imagery of himself running from people wanting to inject him with needles. He was scared to death of needles. So he ran to escape his worst fear.

Power states influence our biological states. I remember the case of the fourteen-year-old girl who was taken against her will into the desert by a rapist. He tortured her and cut off both of her arms. Left to bleed to death, the girl thought of *The Bionic Woman,* a television show in which a woman with artificial limbs had super powers. With that power state serving as her inspiration, this courageous girl did not lie down and wait to die. Instead, she walked fifteen miles and got help.

Personality power states can be summoned up from whatever imagery you dream up. Note the significance of "up," as in onward and upward and "Get up off your rear and put it in gear!" Whether it takes visions of a Bionic Woman, Wonder Woman, or wolverine, the important thing is that you take responsibility for developing your gifts to the fullest and your brain's powers to their maximum potential. These power states of consciousness are tremendous resources. And the greatest thing about them is that they come from within you! That's right, you have all you need to succeed. It is "up" to you!

Eight

OVERCOMING THE EMOTIONAL TRAPS THAT DRAIN YOUR GENIUS

Ten-year-old J.B. had a mild case of attention deficit disorder but a more serious case of lost potential. His parents, who were high achievers themselves, had decided that his three-years-older brother, G.F., was going to be the family genius. Worse yet for J.B., his seven-year-old sister was also a whiz kid and known as the smartest girl in her school. So J.B. was trapped in a cage of high expectations. His father was determined that all of his children would be academic stars. He raised the bar for them every day. Sadly, the father's primary motivation was that he wanted to be able to tell his own parents and siblings that each of his children had earned a Ph.D.

J.B.'s mother also had very high expectations for her children. She was a member of Mensa, and she wanted them to qualify too. Even the children's games were designed to prepare them for academic and intellectual challenges. On car trips, the father or mother would ask questions and the children would compete with each other to give the answer. J.B. did not participate. He had his own "game" going.

When I interviewed his family, J.B. was slow to answer my questions. He waited for his parents to answer for him, something they did all too eagerly. His parents did not understand how pitting their children against each other was unfair to J.B., whose mild ADHD only slightly inhibited his ability to compete, but nonetheless embarrassed him. When J.B. was tested, his brain scan showed a mild slowing in the frontal lobe, but he was able to function quite well. He could perform intellectual tasks without stressing and scored above average on everything except timed tests. He needed encouragement, because if he did not see the answer immediately he would give up. Still, he adapted and improved. He was very outgoing when away from his family. The moment a parent appeared, he went silent and withdrew.

By the end of the second day of testing it was obvious that J.B. shut down when his family was there to answer for him. In private, I asked him what he wanted to be when he grew up. He replied, "I want to be a bank robber and go to prison because I would not have to go to college, and it wouldn't be my fault."

After a pause to see if there was any further explanation, I responded, "Have you ever seen the inside of a prison? I have, and I don't think you would want to pay the price of not being able to go to college. Or do you want someone else to make your decisions for you?"

The question caught him by surprise. He pondered it, perhaps hoping that if he waited long enough I would run out of patience.

Finally he spoke. "I guess I am going to hope someone makes the decisions because I am not smart enough."

He wiped away a tear. I waited.

Finally he said, "I guess I don't know how to answer your question."

I looked into his eyes and said, "Do you want to stay miserable in that safe trap or do you want to learn how to make your own decisions even if it is a little scary?"

Again, a long silence ensued. Then he began to smile. "Do you think my folks would let me?"

J.B. lived a dual life, one within the confines of his family and one in his secret space. When we worked with him alone he was clear and rational, often asserting himself into very complex problem-solving situations gracefully. He began to enjoy his intelligence. But we never saw this sparkle with his family around, which worried all of us.

Three months later I received this letter:

Dr. Lawlis,
I want to thank you for a wonderful time at the PNP Center, and I
remembered what you asked me. I know what you meant, and I
could see you were disappointed when I ducked under my family. But

*you need to know that this is a game, and I am tricking them. I
would have told you but you might have told my parents and they
would know. But I know what I want to be when I grow up, a psychologist like you.*

J.B.

I hope J.B. knows that his fear of success will be a major challenge to
his development and self-recognition. This boy made a deal with his
devil. He purposely disappeared under the radar screen in order to
maintain a family dynamic. As long as he plays this game, he will never
know peace.

THE DANGERS OF STRESS

Stress produces a major hormone called cortisol. High levels of this hormone will alter the brain and put it in survival mode. Then the only focus becomes fight or flight. You are looking either to escape the situation
or to find a weapon to defeat the enemy. These instincts serve humans
well when there are dangerous threats present such as hurricanes coming, burglars in the house, or grizzly bears in the campground. But
when we churn up those fight-or-flight responses because of the internal
threat of stress, we risk moving into a chronic state of anxiety, which is a
killer of a different sort.

Cortisol and a host of other adrenal-stimulating biochemicals basically
block the restoration phase in our bodies because our organs are trapped
in an exhausting state of intense alert. When this becomes chronic, our
tissues disintegrate. One of the leading causes of cardiovascular disease is
high levels of inflammation in the blood. Inflammation is an immune
system response to an injury. The blood thickens with coagulant so that it
clots faster, making strokes and other problems with blood circulation
more probable. The immune system looks around for the enemy and
may start attacking healthy tissues, causing autoimmune diseases to develop, such as arthritis, multiple sclerosis, and lupus. Without stress-free
periods in which the body can restabilize, the body deteriorates. Under
constant stress, brain functions shut down and depression robs the mind
of passion and joy.

Yet we are not good at creating peaceful times for ourselves. We learn how to "stress out" at early ages and we get damned good at it. Just watch any Little League baseball game. Or any junior high volleyball game. Or a Pee Wee football game. Parents pass the stress on to their children, and children share it with each other. A friend recently told me that his fifteen-year-old daughter had to break off a friendship that was ruined by stress. Her longtime girl buddy had become so stressed out by schoolwork and her parents' expectations that she could no longer function normally. She had tremors in the car on the way to school in the morning, and she often threw up at school. You can break it down into shame, ridicule, unrealistic expectations, or threats: no matter what form it takes, most parents will defend and justify their actions as necessary. Most will claim that they are supportive. But their kids are visibly stressed.

Now, it should be understood that stress can be a good thing and a useful tool. To be successful you have to raise your stress levels. While there is an optimal stress level that helps the brain focus, enduring high stress for extended periods only serves to create greater challenges. You lose focus, you lose coordination, and you lose your balance for the real things that count in life. The biggest loss is peace of mind.

I love sports and competition, so I am not against athletics. But things have gotten out of hand. Time and again, I see parents urging their children to "try harder," implying that they are lazy, as if the poor kids were not stressed enough. A parent once told me that he grew angry with his child's performance in school because the child did not look stressed enough. No one who truly understands the impact of stress should want that for a child. Believe me, they'll get it soon enough.

In one family I worked with, a boy had taken his mother's car and wrecked it. As we ended the session, I noted that the mother was not satisfied. When I asked if the measures we had discussed appeared appropriate, her response was, "Yes, but he doesn't look stressed enough. I want him to feel bad, really bad."

Where did people get the idea that stress was desirable for a child? Sure, it's great if the kid needs a rush of adrenaline to escape an attack, a burning building, or a saber tooth tiger, but, parents, daily doses of stress are not conducive to your child's long-term health. Stress is an epidemic. And popping pills is a cure that can be worse than the disease.

ARE YOUR MENTAL CAPACITIES CHALLENGED BY LACK OF PEACE?

Listen up! (Are you feeling stressed yet?) I have created a stress questionnaire to help increase your awareness about the dangers of stress and the benefits of peace of mind for optimal mental functioning. Simply answer these true-or-false questions. I'll even reduce the stress by giving you a third "Sometimes True" (ST) option.

PEACE-NEEDS QUESTIONNAIRE

1. I feel that the circumstances of my life are out of control.

   T　　　ST　　　F

2. I think that others have life better than I do.

   T　　　ST　　　F

3. I have thoughts or worries that continue to stay in my head regardless of how much I want to think about something else.

   T　　　ST　　　F

4. I have trouble concentrating on problems.

   T　　　ST　　　F

5. I find myself daydreaming a lot.

   T　　　ST　　　F

6. I get tired and lose energy quickly.

   T　　　ST　　　F

7. I am a victim of how my family raised me as a child.

   T　　　ST　　　F

8. When I try to solve my problems I get overwhelmed and
   usually give up, hoping that someone smarter than
   I am will help.

   T   ST   F

9. When I get overwhelmed with problems, I self-medicate by eating
   nurturing foods, like sugar- and salt-filled things.

   T   ST   F

10. When I have problems I like to avoid them by watching television,
    going out to parties, etc.

    T   ST   F

11. There are no solutions to my problems.

    T   ST   F

12. I cannot stop worrying about my problems.

    T   ST   F

13. I am either up working and scurrying around or I am sleeping,
    nothing in between.

    T   ST   F

14. My body is usually in pain—stomachaches, headaches,
    backaches, joint aches.

    T   ST   F

15. I don't like doing new things.

    T   ST   F

Scoring:

For the items above, give a credit of 2 for each T (true) and 1 for each ST (sometimes true). Total your credits for a range between 0 and 30, and compare your score to the ranges below:

Total Score	Interpretation
22–30	This score represents the maximum negative impact on your mental activities. You are allowing stress to tremendously interfere with your mental capacities, and you may actually be creating many of your own challenges.
15–21	You need more peace in your mental activities, which will make you more efficient in dealing with problems.
9–14	You are in need of a more peaceful state of mind. This would enable you to release much of the mental baggage that is sabotaging your life's goals.
4–8	Your life appears to be relatively well balanced, however, there are areas that you need to address that would be helpful in achieving success.
0–3	There is little indication that you may have psychological barriers for continued intellectual growth.

THE TWO BASIC SPHERES OF CRITICAL PEACE

Fear and ambivalence are instinctive emotional responses. Even infants express fear with the "startle reflex," in which the arms are thrown up if the child senses he is falling or he is suddenly frightened. Our responses to fear become more sophisticated as we mature. But it can still paralyze us and block us from achieving our dreams. Often, we find ways to minimize the pain we anticipate when fear strikes. But those "games" only further sabotage our dreams in most cases.

J.B. acted incompetent to minimize the pain of rejection. Yet his little game also sabotaged his success, and robbed him of any peace of mind. His "game" became a full-time job.

There are seven basic fears most people experience. Rate each of these descriptions in terms of their relevance to your basic fears on a scale of 1 (no relevance) to 10 (high relevance).

- Inability to survive: This fear could mean death, but more often it means the loss of the means to survive. The leading fear among new millionaires is the fear of being a "bag person." Rating: (1–10) _____

- Insecurity: This fear often relates to issues of abandonment or a dependence on a trust that was broken. This fear is most often seen in marriage problems where the relationship cannot assuage it. Rating: (1–10) _____

- Loss of love: This fear may be more specifically the fear of being unworthy of love. Rating: (1–10) _____

- Loss of self-esteem: This fear can be pronounced when esteem is based on external factors, such as money, power, or family status. Rating: (1–10) _____

- Powerlessness: This fear can be seen often when a person cannot express their emotional needs in relationships. Rating: (1–10) _____

- Loss of self-control: This fear is very pronounced among the elderly and with the possibility of dementia, but it is also very relevant to those who fear that anxiety or depression will overwhelm their abilities to function and be productive. Rating: (1–10) _____

- Insignificance: This fear is related to the loss of a reason to keep living and meeting the challenges of life's circumstances. Without a vision of your personal contribution to someone or something, you can lose yourself. Rating: (1–10) _____

The higher your score, the more likely it is that you are locked in a state of ambivalence. Appropriate fear helps protect you from danger, but irrational fears will sabotage your dreams and rob you of any peace. Ambivalence is like being stuck in neutral because you don't know whether to go forward or backward. It also interferes with your ability to control your destiny. Eli got stuck in neutral because he wanted to become a chef, but he also wanted to please his parents, who felt he should become musical director of their church. Or consider Jonas, who claimed that he wanted to be his own boss, but he also wanted job security. He too got stuck in neutral.

No one can do it all. No one can have it all. We must decide what we are willing to dedicate our lives to, and then relinquish other options.

Use the following exercise to evaluate your own ambivalences.

Step One:

Write down your top ten priorities for your goals in life. Include relationship (marriage and family), vocational success, prestige, love, and any other aspects you want to consider in this list.

1.

2.

3.

4.

5.

6.

7.

8.

9.

10.

Step Two:

The next step is to decide which of these priorities you could live without. Merely cross out those you consider noncritical to whatever definition you have for your life's work. You may still want these elements, but you are willing to release them for the sake of achieving the others.

Step Three:

Rank in order the remaining elements to determine your top requirement, then your second requirement, and so on. This is your life goal priority list, and this is what it means.

My clinical experience shows that you have a 90 percent probability of achieving your top choice, and a 15 percent chance of achieving your second priority; however, this drops to 1 percent if it is in conflict with the first. Your third choice is a probable 5 percent, but that would be a maximum—again, if not in direct conflict with the other two. The reason I can say this confidently is because there is a human law about the investment your brain can make in a given goal. It is limited because your time and energy are limited. Any conflict or ambivalence dissipates the available amount of both.

There is good and bad news to this assessment. The good news is that you can achieve just about any goal you want as long as there is focus. You could make a million dollars (honestly), lose a hundred pounds of fat, get a Ph.D., or marry the mayor's beautiful daughter, but the bad news is that you can't do it all at once. You have to commit to one priority. Ambivalence is not allowed.

MYTHS OF POWER AND THE GAMES WE PLAY

The traps of fear may be relatively easy to see. We all have baggage. No one goes through this life without falling into some traps. It is the development of skills to get out of those traps that is tough. When we fall into those traps, we lose the ability to exercise the full power of our brains. We limit our opportunities and fall off the path to our dreams. When we invent games to avoid pain or fear, we still sabotage our success. It's just another trap, only one of our own making. You need to recognize both the traps and the games so that you remain in control of your destiny.

The basic mythical strategies we use to protect ourselves from fear are: *revenge, power struggle, attention getting,* and *incompetence.*

Revenge is an indirect reaction to fear of loss of power. The perceived redemptive quality of vengeance is really a myth. The myth is that once you get revenge you will feel at peace. Doesn't happen. You do not resolve anxiety with vengeful action. Even bringing a killer to justice doesn't make up for the loss of life. As one family member of a murder victim noted, "I thought I would feel better, but I don't." Even the execution of such criminals hasn't brought peace.

A *power struggle* is a confrontation to resolve the turmoil that disrupts inner peace. It is manifested as the "blaming game," in which someone or something becomes the target of our fears and ambivalences. I am director of after-care for the guests on *Dr. Phil.* I work with Anthony Haskins, my coordinator, to fulfill Dr. Phil's promises to the guests. If he says that his show will provide for long-term counseling services after the cameras stop rolling, it is our job to follow through and deliver on that promise. It is a big responsibility, and it can get complex. We sometimes become the targets of the blame game. Sometimes we are targeted even for things that have little to do with what happens on the show. We once had a call from a father who made threats because he could not find his son. It seems the father sent his son to a camping program that was advertised on a channel that carried *Dr. Phil.* Since *Dr. Phil* came on that channel each day, this guy felt Dr. Phil and his people (me) should know where his son was. We did try to help him find his son, but it would have been illegal for the camp authorities to release information to us. This father focused his sense of injustice on the show, not on his own fears.

This father's outrage is a good example of a power struggle because of his misplaced target. Power struggles are rarely between two people; rather, they are misplaced fears of a person's own struggles. Other parties are usually only easy targets. The most common power struggles are the fights people have with their parents. Many adults still blame their parents for their problems. They don't seem to understand that even if their parents failed them in some way, it does no good to keep blaming them. It will bring no relief for their fears, no end to their ambivalence, and no peace. The only solution is forgiveness of self and correct communication.

Attention getting is the attempt to find peace through recognition and productivity. This is the game of "look at me," in which we attempt to place an overlay of accomplishment over our deepest fears. A patient, Isaac, felt insecure about his mother's love because of her narrow focus on his academic performance. He'd spent a good part of his life trying to win his mother's attention in other ways. He didn't get what he needed by riding his bicycle with no hands. He didn't get it by becoming a masterful pianist. He had an obsessive fear that his mother would one day forget him.

I met him in a pain clinic where he was a patient in the rehabilitation program. He suffered from severe back spasms. The case was complex because there was no clear cause for his problems. He'd already undergone a spinal operation that did not relieve the symptoms. What was fascinating to me was the fact that Isaac never took a day off from work, except for medical leave. He was perpetually concerned about the performance of his unit and called in every day.

In a group session in which patients talked about their fears, Isaac explained his issues. Two group members questioned him about the source of his pain, fears, and ambivalences. Isaac came to realize the origins of his fears. A very bright guy, he saw that he'd fallen into a trap and he realized he needed to get on a new path to improve his health.

In private sessions we explored Isaac's fears and, without really addressing the pain itself, he dropped his game and began to create more insightful and clearer goals. The pain resolved itself within five weeks, but the symptom was not important, and it was not discussed because it probably existed at an unconscious level. It was the seat of the cause that mattered.

The game of *incompetence* is a major problem for many people. They simply learn that incompetence pays off. This is often called "learned helplessness." This scenario usually starts off in childhood when a child learns to display helplessness so someone else will take responsibility. That "someone" is usually a rescuer playing another game. My own version of this sprang from my dislike of washing the dishes. I would dawdle on the process, loitering around the kitchen, gobbling leftovers. I wasted time, but worse, I left messes on the plates and pans. I would rewash a dish several times when it was pointed out, because the sacrifice was worth it. I won. I was declared incompetent as a dishwasher and relieved of that duty. That small victory resulted in the assignment of cleaning the toilets. I discovered that cleaning dishes is not the nastiest of jobs after all. After a lot of whining and more gaming, I got my dishwashing job back. Life returned to a more peaceful routine away from the toilet bowl.

Learned helplessness can also be played out as alcohol and drug addictions, obesity, chronic pain, and even eating disorders. These habits grow into critical diseases when taken to the extreme. Still, it all boils down to people avoiding responsibility for their own lives and their own peace and happiness.

STEPS TO PEACE: A THREE-DIMENSIONAL PROGRAM

Very few people really even know how it feels to be relaxed. The majority of Americans are stress-laden. There are no curricula, no schools or television shows that teach us effective ways for achieving inner peace. Too often the noise and distractions of daily worries and fears drain our emotional energy. But there are steps to peace, proven over time and across cultures. Peace and harmony are essential to emotional well-being.

I've developed a program for learning that process. Reading about it will get you started, and if you want to follow up, my relaxation CDs are available at Mindbodyseries.com. There are also other excellent relaxation or biofeedback therapists who offer direct training. There are no negative side effects to seeking peace.

The peace-making program is a four-phase process:

1. Deepening the paths to peace skills

2. Identifying the challenges to peace

3. Identifying and applying the resources within

4. Finding and using the resources from the external world

1. Deepening the Paths to Peace Skills

You have already been introduced to breathing approaches for stimulating various parts of your brain. I want to review some specific paths to peace via the relaxation process. There are some promises you have to make in order for you to get past first base. You can't just decide to find peace. This is a lifestyle. It requires commitment. You must:

Find thirty minutes to relax each day. This must be a priority, not something you squeeze in when all of your work is done. This may be the toughest requirement of all, but if you cannot do it, you have wasted your time.

Designate a quiet place where you cannot be disturbed, except in a national emergency or an approaching hurricane. The place should be free of distractions (no television, no radio, no audible discussions from others, no phone, etc.). If you want soothing music, it should have no lyrics and preferably no strong melodies. Some people burn candles and those are fine but not necessary.

Find a physical position in which there is a minimum of muscle tension. Some sit in a cross-legged position to keep the spine straight. The best relaxation processing I know involves lying in a lounge chair or sitting against the wall for support. Clothing should be loose and comfortable.

As you enter into your peaceful period, it will be hard at first because of the foreign sense of releasing all other thoughts and activities. Therefore, be clear to yourself that this period is for you.

The first path to inner peace is the integration of breathing techniques. Feel yourself breathing. Only breathing. It might be helpful to focus on cycling your breath to your pulse or heartbeat so that the length of each out-breath is the same as your in-breath. If you are comfortable with three beats of your heart for each breath, then you breathe in for three heartbeats and out in three heartbeats. It may be easier to change those cycles as you relax, but concentration and focus are the most important things.

Maintain your breathing patterns for at least twenty minutes. Allow your body to follow the same pattern of breathing, relaxing more and more with each breath. You will have difficulty maintaining this concentration for more than two minutes at first because your brain is not used to this lack of clutter. I find that every time a thought or worry comes into my mind, instead of trying to resist it, I allow it to pass through my mind without processing it. It is like a sailboat that silently sails across your mind without changing its course.

If you lose concentration or get bored, reenter the state and do not give up. This practice alone will take you into a state of peace.

The second path to peace is more active and easier too. It involves using whatever imagery works for you—not just visual imagery, but also other sensory mediums. It is easier for most people to recall sounds, such as music or soothing prayers, and to remember the soft touches of massage and comforting experiences. Perhaps the most easily retrieved sensory experience is that of smell, such as remembering the smell of flowers or other items. The smells of jasmine, lavender, and roses are famous for their power to induce relaxation. The scent of someone who comforts you is also a powerful aid.

You can create your own imagery by allowing your mind to wander. Note that when you are "traveling" you must not stop for long in any one place. Don't let your past obsessions interfere or interrupt. My favorite visualization is to take a journey through the middle of the earth or to fly in the sky.

Sometimes it may be helpful to use good memories for your imagery. Listening to ocean waves or rain on the roof can be a very powerful relaxation aid. Cuddling in a soft bed, lying on a raft on the water, or swinging in a hammock round out the top five choices in my office. Playing in warm mud seems to be a favorite with younger people. Some individuals have used the memories of deep medicated experiences as guides, as well as recreational medications.

The imagery trips can be enjoyable and educational as well. You may find that certain symbols, such as colors, smells, and animals, serve as powerful agents for insights. It is true that your mind can heal if given time with you alone.

2. Identifying the Challenges to Peace

You have already identified some of the obstacles to your peace through your assessments of fears and ambivalences. This is like facing your demons and seeing their vulnerabilities. It is critical that you attempt this when you are relaxed or it might heighten your anxiety. When you feel comfortable, confront your worst fear. If you feel yourself getting stressed, back out of the imagery. Go back to your relaxation state and wait for a while.

The practice of being able to confront your fears gives you two important tools. The most important one is that you learn that you can back out from these fears, you can control your mind and what you want to think about. The second feature is that hopefully you see your fears are not that horrible. They are more frightening when you avoid them than when you confront them.

This may sound contrary to your concept of peace, but trust me, you can eliminate these demons pretty fast when you see them as mostly figments. But some of them are real-life fears. For example, one of my patients, Frank, had AIDS. His greatest fear was death. As he entered his deepest relaxation, he faced death in the symbol of a black spider. As he maintained his relaxation, he began to feel the deepest calm and peace. The spider was not to be feared, he reasoned, it was merely a time in which there would be no fears at all. It would be a wonderful time when he could simply be free of any expectations or threats. The spider was only a symbol of pain with no real powers. Even when he approached it there was no movement of the spider. He brushed the black hairs and discovered a calming effect. As he continued to stroke the spider, it melted into a kitten. Frank discovered that if he could stroke his fears, they would melt into something he loved.

Frank's experiences began to shift his focus on life as well. He relaxed and found peace in the midst of his disease. He learned to love his symbols. It was rather amazing to see the glow around this young man's face as he walked through the door to my office. Interestingly, Frank is still alive and well today. His AIDS went into remission, and although there is always concern, he appears to have been given a new birth.

3. Identifying and Applying the Resources Within

Hopefully you have gained a few skills for finding peace at this point. You have discovered breathing techniques, exercises to promote peace, and even music to move you in the right direction. This is another application of your imagery. You can make yourself your own hero. This is empowerment that comes from peace and love instead of threat and insecurity. You may use your fantasy heroes like Spider-Man or Batman, a powerful animal symbol, or whatever symbol that comes to you. Repeat this motto: *Out of peace comes the best of me.*

We all exist on the basis of love and protection. Each cell in your body has been carefully engineered beyond the level of understanding of any scientist to protect you at all costs. Your hormones, your blood cells, your total being rests on the fact that you are a unique being. The entire structure of your body and mind serves your purposes, and it is done with devotion.

My respected physicist friends believe there is no rational reason why the atoms that make up our bodies hang together to form the wonder that is us. Imagine how much it would cost the government to build you from scratch. Each atom hangs with the others for one reason: its devotion to you. Pretty amazing! The forty miles of nerves and the four hundred miles of blood vessels form an incredible creation, yet the cost for the raw materials (calcium, magnesium, etc.) would run about $1.85.

You are an amazing structure. You have strengths built into your mind and body that have yet to be tapped. There are secrets to running this body you have yet to understand. You can begin to think of yourself as the marvel that you are. You are priceless.

As you contemplate the power you have at your control, imagine the source of your strength and bring in that symbol of power. If you can imagine a symbol of God, perhaps in the form of a human or even in more symbolic forms (the cross, the Star of David, the sword, etc.), imagine it with you and feel the surge of power. With such power you cannot be defeated. Your body might take a beating, but nothing can touch your spirit. Embrace the glory of yourself. You have the power to overcome your fear of anything and anyone.

This high energy comes not from violence but from your sense of inner peace and wisdom. The power is yours as long as you trust in it. This is peace of mind and clarity of purpose.

4. Finding and Using the Resources from the External World

You probably have some resources that give you a sense of peace. Now is the time to embrace these and incorporate them into your sense of self. Make a list of sources that bring you into a deeper peaceful state. Create a set of empowerment tools. Create a pie chart of those acts or items that you value as parts of a totally centered and balanced life. Consider the following examples as parts of your peaceful state:

1. Walking on long strolls with your dog

2. Listening to Mozart or Jonn Serrie

3. Dancing with your lover

4. Being held by your lover

5. Drinking chamomile tea

6. Sitting on the beach, feeling the sun, and listening to the ocean waves as they come onto the beach

7. Praying

8. Holding a baby in your arms

9. Having a massage

10. Singing sacred songs

11. Playing a flute

12. Writing a letter to a great friend

After making the list, draw a pie chart and adjust the amount of space in accordance with how much that particular source offers you peace. For example, I will fill in the pie chart in accordance with how much each element appears to enhance my own sense of peace.

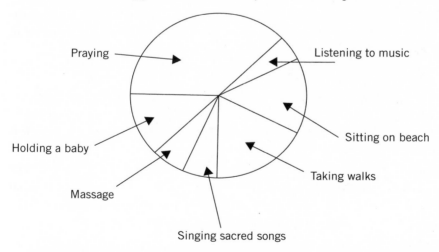

The pie chart you produced is your "peace pie." Use it as a reminder of those things that give you a sense of peace. You can use these elements to mobilize peace. These major ones do not black out others not yet mentioned, but they help you grasp your most powerful tools. You can integrate them into your formula for a total life balance. The search will continue for life because different elements will bring peace according to the nature of your circumstances. But never give up your peace because that is what brings true happiness and self-fulfillment.

OVERVIEW

Negative energy robs you of creativity and joy. The good news is that you can break out of your bondage to fear and ambivalence. It takes courage to face the demons, and it takes courage to look at your true self. You may have anxiety, depression, post-traumatic stress disorder, attention deficit disorder, or a half dozen other symptoms, but these are things that have *happened* to you. They do not *define* you. If you have cancer, it does not mean that you *are* cancer. There is no fear in having something wrong with you because there are more things right with you.

Suffering is for victims. Survivors fight. You are a victim only when you accept that mantle. You don't have to accept it. You are free to walk away from it. Use the tools I've introduced, and find peace in the knowledge that they don't come from me. You have always had these skills. I am only a messenger.

Nine

RIGHT THINKING

The first time I saw thirteen-year-old Chanice slouched in our waiting room chair with her *Don't mess with me* attitude, I knew she was a candidate for my "Yahoo" approach to troubled kids.

Her parents brought this pretty girl to us because her grades had taken a nosedive over the last two years. She'd gone from straight A's to C's and D's. Her parents were reasonably upset. They blamed her lack of motivation for her problems in school. They thought of her as lazy and "boy crazy," and they were seriously considering an all-girls academy for the next year.

She did wear enough makeup to coat all of the Dallas Cowboys cheerleaders. And she was dressed in an ensemble that must have been bohemian chic, but looked to me like Salvation Army.

My bet was that Chanice was a whole lot smarter than her recent report cards indicated. So, I aimed high.

"Well, Chanice, you certainly have your parents in a frenzy, but I am wondering if that is what you want right now."

She seemed puzzled by my statement, and definitely ready to rumble.

"What do you mean? Aren't you going to psychoanalyze me and tell them that I need counseling? I can tell you some really bad things I've done, and you will give them the information to pack me away. Is that what you want me to do?"

I looked at her with a grin and responded, "No, I will probably tell them that you are smarter than that because both of us know you are. But I am curious what you do want me to tell them."

After a long stare, I got the full 'tude.

"Are you for real?" she said. "I would like for you to tell them that they make me so mad that I want to quit school altogether. Tell them that they have driven me to the point that I don't want to be their daughter anymore. They have hurt me so much that I want them to hurt as much as I do."

"So you want me to hurt them for you. Is that right?"

Chanice nodded in agreement while she wiped away her tears. "They just make me look so bad to my friends, and they have pushed me away from them with all their big plans for me."

"So how did they do that?"

The makeup was running down her cheeks, making her look like a clown.

"They want me to be different from my friends. They even call them lazy or stupid because they are not as smart as I am. I am supposed to be a lawyer, you know, and make good grades, practice my piano, and be the top in my class. Can you imagine how that feels?"

"What I can imagine is that you feel that your family hurts your feelings and makes you act the way you do because they want you to be a different person and expect you to want the same things they want for you. Is that close to how you feel?"

Chanice looked me in the eye and said:

"Yes, you see how bad they make me feel?"

"And you want to make them feel bad, too?" I said.

She nodded wildly as she wiped and smeared her makeup more. "And the money they spent on this session would be worth that to you?"

Apparently so. We had a plan.

"Okay, what we have to do is to make your parents feel bad, so how do you suppose we do that? This is a real tough question, Chanice, because I can't make anyone think what I want them to think. They obviously can't make you think the way they want you to think, and you can't hurt their feelings by your activities. I don't think this is going to work any better than what you have tried so far. I guess I have to give your money back."

Chanice was puzzled. "You are a psychologist. Shouldn't you know what to do?"

"No one—not me nor anyone else—can make a person think in specific ways. I am really glad because you can imagine how the world would be, can't you? Let's just roll old Chanice through Dr. Lawlis's office and do a head shrink on her and get her shaped up. Do you think that is why you are here?"

"Yes, I do. Isn't it?"

"Well, do you think I could change your thinking so you would start studying again for your parents' pleasure? I think not, because you are so intent on hurting them that you are willing to sell your soul to the devil, so to speak. I don't think anyone could do that, because you are too smart and strong for that. But you may be hurting yourself more than you are hurting them. I guess that is your choice—to try and hurt them or to help yourself," I said.

"They are making me do these things," she replied.

"No, Chanice, no one can make you think anything. That is always your choice as to how you react. You can always choose your reactions, and they may be good or bad, depending on what your ultimate goals are."

Then I hit her with my Yahoo Thinking Principle. "Yahoo" stands for *You Always Have Other Options*. I told Chanice that she had other options for dealing with her parents.

"But always remember that the best options in your thinking should be consistent with your dreams and goals for what you want," I said.

After Chanice understood her range of choices and her power to determine her own future, she resolved to build a new relationship with her parents. Instead of being "Little Miss Rebel," she followed a proactive plan that set her on course to her goals. This included negotiating a contract to study 60 percent of the time and then to play with friends 40 percent of the time. Her parents agreed not to criticize her as long as the house rules and values were upheld.

Chanice's plan did work. But it was not the plan that freed her for more productive thinking and problem solving. It was the fact that she realized she had *control* over her thinking. I taught her that she had the power to choose how she responded to her parents. She learned that she had a shield. She could decide how to let the words of others affect her. She could accept feedback or not.

She learned to evaluate and assess the world around her and determine her own reality rather than let other people push her buttons. She found that she could open herself to the joys of living.

BECOME THE CAPTAIN OF YOUR SHIP WITH RIGHT THINKING

Our emotional peace relies on our internal thinking. Too often we are our own worst enemy. By correcting wrong thinking patterns, you are free to accomplish goals in all areas of your life. The statements below represent the most basic of "thinking" principles. They have far-reaching implications.

We are in direct control of our emotional intelligence. We have been conditioned as to what is "bad" and "good" behavior. Our parents, teachers, bosses, and Madison Avenue tell us what we "should" do. We risk shame and embarrassment if we do not drink the right beer, drive the right car, and wear the right clothes. The news threatens death and disaster every minute. There are serious threats, for sure, but the hype overshadows the truth much of the time.

In his book *The Gift of Fear,* Gavin De Becker reinforces the idea that we need to give more credibility to our intuitions about potentially harmful situations. There is no external force possible that can "make" us feel in a specific way. We cannot change the world, but we can change the way we feel about what happens in the world and how we respond to it.

It sounds almost preposterous to say that we are in direct control of our internal world. Yet, even those who are imprisoned have the freedom to choose their responses. Viktor Frankl noted that when he was a prisoner during World War II, the prisoners who gave in to the horrors of the external world died most quickly. Those who chose to maintain peace within survived.

It is not others who "make" us afraid, angry, or even happy. That power resides within. We can react to the injustices as we choose. We may want to feel justified or victimized, but what good does that do? Many individuals feel that pain is a way of cleansing their thoughts. They think torturing themselves will relieve anxieties. They are wrong.

You have control of your reactions to the forces that play upon you. And so, scary as it may be, we are responsible for how we think and especially how we respond to outside influences, whether it is white Afrikaners mocking us in a South African prison, racists outside a Birmingham school, or Roman soldiers forcing us to wear a crown of thorns. We all have the power to reject their ways and follow our own.

How we perceive and respond internally to external influence depends largely on the internal dialogue we generate. Our "two brains" give us the gift of self-reflection, which means that we have the wonderful ability to monitor our inner thoughts and to conduct inner conversations. This is also known as "the voice inside your head" or your conscience. This has often been depicted as the debate between our "good" and our "bad" sides. Freud described the dueling little devils on each shoulder as the *id* and the *superego*.

Internal dialogue produces not mischief, but rather rationality and clarity. It is the truth we possess about ourselves and the world that increases or decreases the quality of our thinking as well as the quality of our lives. And it is certainly not the "masculine" definition of rational thought—narrow compartmental processes of deductive or inductive reasoning—that represents psychological power. Although there is justification for learning logical reasoning concepts, what's most important is how well we know ourselves, our biases, and the naked reality we face.

We have different patterns of thinking. We all think in different modes. We honor those who think creatively and for the benefit of all. We revere spiritual leaders and their great wisdom. We adore actors for the roles they play that symbolize aspects of our lives.

There are many effective thinking styles, and most of them work very well for mental health. Some people are better visual thinkers, and some are better with auditory thinking styles. Some are better emotional thinkers, and others are better in technical realms. The greatest thinkers in history had diverse interests and talents. Leonardo da Vinci studied war and weapons as well as art. Einstein studied music and physics. Multiple paths usually cultivate different areas of the brain.

ARE YOU USING RIGHT THINKING PROCESSING?

We can be fooled by our own egos, especially when we feel that our way of thinking and reacting has worked in the past. I remember one person in particular who thought that his wealth made him an authority beyond reproach. His fortune was made as a real estate speculator. He got in the game at the right time, in the right place. But he was convinced of his genius. He eventually went bankrupt, and then to jail, losing his wife and his possessions. My point is that you cannot judge your efficiency of thinking by your economic or professional circumstances. Sometimes, you just get lucky.

This questionnaire helps analyze your "right thinking." Please answer the following items by circling the best response to each: Always True (AT), Sometimes True (ST), Rarely True (RT), or Never True (NT).

1. When I try to make decisions I am always worried that I will hurt someone's feelings.

   AT   ST   RT   NT

2. I believe that for every question there is a basic answer that can be agreed upon by everyone.

   AT   ST   RT   NT

3. In my deepest desire I want everyone to like and respect me for what I think.

   AT   ST   RT   NT

4. It bothers me when someone disagrees with me, especially a close friend or a family member.

   AT   ST   RT   NT

5. I am hesitant to voice my judgment on any decision because I do not have the education others have.

   AT   ST   RT   NT

6. I was abused as a child so I am destined to make poor decisions in my life.

   AT   ST   RT   NT

7. My parents always told me that I was a misfit or abnormal, and I believed them.

    AT   ST   RT   NT

8. When I am not being productive, I feel guilty because my worth is based on what I do, not what I say.

    AT   ST   RT   NT

9. I base my decisions on what I consider as fact, and the fact is that I am a loser.

    AT   ST   RT   NT

10. I do what people expect me to do because I have a role to play and I play it well.

    AT   ST   RT   NT

11. I believe that fun and joy are privileges that I might deserve to have only periodically.

    AT   ST   RT   NT

12. I have done some bad things that can never be forgiven, and my internal shame is my burden to bear.

    AT   ST   RT   NT

13. I do not trust people.

    AT   ST   RT   NT

14. I have several major flaws of my body and face, which make me unappealing and unattractive.

    AT   ST   RT   NT

15. I spend a lot of time regretting my decisions of the past because I am paying the price now.

AT   ST   RT   NT

Scoring:

For each rating of Always True (AT) assign a value of 4 points, for each rating of Sometimes True (ST) assign a value of 2 points, and for each rating of Rarely True (RT) assign a value of 1 point. Total the values for a score from 0 to 60, and compare your score with the general interpretations below:

40–60   Your thinking patterns are seriously affected by destructive processing patterns. You need to carefully train yourself into more constructive and more powerful thinking patterns.

30–39   Your thinking patterns are more focused on your negative self-image than on effective informational processing.

20–29   Your thinking patterns reflect some strong interference from early formulations of how you learned to think and immature concepts about your worth.

10–19   Your thinking patterns are confused in some specific areas. This is probably due to the uncertainties of your lack of self-esteem and a need for others to agree with you.

0–9   Your thinking patterns are the least affected by your need for self-esteem and external validities; however, any rating greater than zero is probably a sign that you could improve on some levels of your thinking abilities.

The basis for assessing your thinking is that most of us grow up thinking there are "right answers." I have always generally considered my father to be the ideal parent. He encouraged me to think on my own. Still, one incident will always stand out. My father sold cars for about ten years of my youth. I enjoyed that period very much. I worked as a mechanic during high school, and I knew a lot about cars. But one of his customers complained that he was hearing bird whistles in his car. I could hear them too. Five of us tried to locate the source. But we couldn't find it until I discovered a dead bird in the radiator. Without telling anyone that I'd found it, I carried the dead bird to a trash can. My father noted what I was doing: "That is not the problem. Throw that thing away."

I released the dead bird and walked out of the shop as I heard another man say, "Hey, it stopped." The other men, including my father, agreed, and the consensus was that it was a mysterious event and if it happened again, to bring the vehicle back for another try. The secret was mine. I had solved the problem. I was smarter than my father or his adult friends. I did not need his validation because I knew without a word that I was right. I remember to this day, over fifty years later, the pride I felt when I knew I could think and solve problems on my own, even if my father did not believe me.

Clear thinking is that isolated process in which you can reach your own conclusion, regardless of social pressure, regardless of the need to be right to others. This is the pattern of constructive problem solving.

THE GOLDEN STANDARD FOR POWERFUL THINKING PATTERNS

These are five basic criteria for right thinking. They are clear standards that you can use to measure every thought in relation to the goals and objectives you have for your life. The basic five criteria are:

- Is your perception fact or fiction?
- Is it in your interest to have this thought?
- Is having this thought serving your purpose or another's?
- Does maintaining this thought harm you physically, mentally, or spiritually?
- Does your thinking advance your goals?

Is Your Perception Fact or Fiction?

It is a truism that we do not "see" or "hear" the world directly. We use our senses to tell us what it looks like, how it feels, and what it sounds like. When we see a flower, what we really perceive is the reflection of light waves that stimulate the tiny nerves in our eyes, the retina. These wave forms are computed through various parts of the brain for interpretation. In a simplified explanation, the first step is through the rear lobe, the occipital lobe, and then it is transmitted to the temporal lobe for memory associations, and then to the frontal lobe for the understanding of the perception. If you had never seen a flower before, this image would make no sense and you might even fear it because it is strange to you.

If we have a fear of flowers our bodies will go into anxiety behaviors. We will tend to use negative language to describe all flowers as "bad, frightening, and dangerous." We will attribute hostile intentions to flowers and live our life in avoidance of them.

Distortion is even greater in those areas where we have partial sensory input. Consider the concept of "cancer." The initial diagnosis of cancer presents a very threatening and powerful image for most of us. Few have actually seen or touched a cancer tumor, much less viewed one from a microscope. When you realize that a cancer cell is pretty vulnerable and does nothing but grow, more rational perceptions can enter your mind and allow you to better manage the disease.

This standard criterion of determining fact over fiction is the first because it may be the most critical. It challenges you to decide if your reality is distorted. Does that person really dislike you, or are you defensive because he or she is smarter or richer than you? Does your teacher really discriminate against you, or are you behaving in such a way that you require more attention? Is the world a bitter, hostile place, or is it a benevolent place with many blessings? Is your glass half empty or half full?

In some images there is no true conclusion of truth, there is just the perceived interpretation of one person versus the interpretation of another. Consider the "man in the moon" phenomenon. Which image

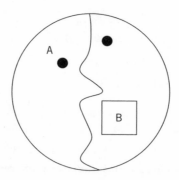

represents the image of the man in the moon for the picture on page 152: A or B? The correct answer could be A, B, A and B, or neither.

Life is rarely fact. The truth depends mostly on what is real to you. The same "truth" may not hold for anyone else, it is also not true that everyone has to agree with your point of view in order for you to be right. It is not true that a person who is better educated than you always has a better answer. It is not a basic truth that everyone has to love you in order for you to be a good person. These are myths that destroy effective thinking because they serve as false axioms.

Is It in Your Interest to Have This Thought?

This criterion serves as a judgment of whether or not it is of value for you to maintain your thoughts. If not, it is your decision. Does it help to hold on to the thought that you were abused as a child? I am not suggesting that we avoid or deny our experiences, but does holding on to this thought have a positive payoff for you? Does holding on to that thought create better opportunities? These are hard questions. You have the ability to discard thoughts. There are toxic thoughts that can poison your thinking.

One way to strip the emotional tones from your thoughts is to use imagery. Think of detaching fear and ambivalence from your life. May, a sixteen-year-old, had a fierce attitude. When asked why she was so angry, she explained that when they were both children her male cousin had teased her after seeing her naked. She had felt strange ever since, and these feelings were ruling her life. If she ever wanted to find peace, she would have to let go of the negative emotions that were no longer serving her.

The decision to release the emotions attached to a memory is a path to forgiveness. This is not a condoning, approval, or even acceptance of past acts or events. It is merely a willingness to release the emotional burden of holding the memory or motivation for revenge or condemnation. May eventually made the choice to release the horror and embarrassment of this past event. She simply relaxed and let go of the anger and despair by seeing herself walk away from it.

I have observed and guided many people through this first stage toward forgiveness. Many had endured horrendous physical and mental abuse. Yet each expressed deep relief and joy when they learned how to release the demons related to the abuse. They realized they had a choice. And every one of them chose joy over pain, anger, or victimization.

Is Having This Thought Serving Your Purpose or Another's?

For most people, it isn't easy to relinquish ownership of a long-held thought, even a self-destructive one. The stories that are created usually spring from the need to control your own situation. The parent's words or criticisms often become magnified in the child's recollection. The negative "self statements" may sound like:

"You are stupid and don't care about doing things right."

"You don't care about anyone else but you. You are selfish."

"You idiot! How many times do I have to tell you . . ."

"You dummy. Anyone with a brain would have done better."

These statements may sound familiar. I hear them every time I walk through the grocery market and listen to parents threaten their children. Fast-forward to postadolescence, and those messages are still playing in the minds of many adults. They thwart their efforts to succeed and find peace. It may defy common sense, but it happens all the time. Criticisms we hear as children can play over and over in our adult minds, undermining our mental capacities, robbing us of as much as 25 to 50 percent of our potential intelligence.

But it doesn't have to be that way. You can control this negative inner dialogue. It requires a sort of reprogramming. The steps have to be consciously followed and practiced.

1. Learn to relax and diminish the negative inner dialogue. During this step you learn how to use the mirror of your mind to become aware of the exact words and tone of the inner dialogue. You need to write them down so you have an immediate consciousness of these statements.

2. Plan for alternative and more rational self-statements. These new statements are substitutes for the negative ones.

3. Practice the substitutions in real life. This can be accomplished in two ways. You can imagine typical situations in which you normally

berate yourself or recall an incident in which the negative internal dialogue played out. The nice thing about using imagery is that you can play it over and practice the alternative internal dialogue. The second way to practice is in actual life situations. You can anticipate them and be ready to unleash the more positive alternative dialogue.

Does Maintaining This Thought Harm You Physically, Mentally, or Spiritually?

Some thoughts are toxic and can cause physical damage to the body. A common example of this is known as "anticipated validation." A child who gets on a bike thinking "I'm going to fall and break my arm" is anticipating failure so that he won't be disappointed, but instead validated, when the crash comes.

If you anticipate failure, it will be more likely to occur. If you expect to fall off your bicycle, you probably will. If you expect to forget all the information you studied during the test, you probably will. The prospect of having some disease is heightened if you expect it.

The mechanism in the brain follows the imagery process. Remember that we only know our world through our senses and our interpretations of those sensations. If we hold on to the idea of those sensations, our bodies do not know the difference. You see this when a hypnotist plants an image in the mind of a subject and they respond as if it were real. If the hypnotist tells the person that she is eating a lemon, she will react to the sour taste.

The process is pretty simple. The imagery stimulates the same neurological network as the actual experience. If you imagine being chased by the police, your body responds. Your hormones call for adrenal stimulation. Your blood pressure rises. Your muscles get tense as the blood flows into them.

Similarly, when you maintain a thought that depletes your physical reserves and makes you vulnerable to disease, you will get sick. Your imagery will help create that probability.

Does Your Thinking Advance Your Goals?

The first step in this criterion is to determine your goals and their priority. I once went to a prosperity seminar on how to make a million dollars.

It was sponsored by the Unity Church of Dallas, Texas. I figured that it was based on a religious philosophy of *abundance,* which was known to be a vital part of that church's central message. It turned out to be more of a neurological explanation of how to succeed in whatever goals you set for yourself.

The central step was to be aware of one goal and match that goal every day with thoughts toward that goal. No negative challenges were tolerated. It was taught that your thoughts with their associated behaviors would eventually move you toward your goals, whether it was a million dollars, weight loss, or marital bliss. My wife and I bought matching used Mercedes cars to demonstrate our faith that we would attain our financial goals. But we failed to understand a critical concept. If the goal is to make a million dollars, you have to save money, not spend it.

By setting specific goals and focusing on them, you develop a lifestyle according to the goals and you set priorities along the way. Opportunities arise because you are more aware of them, and by acting on these thoughts, more of them come to fruition.

EXERCISES FOR RIGHT THINKING

We learn best by doing rather than talking. I have constructed an exercise with real-life situations in which someone might hear destructive internal messages. It might be helpful for you to complete these exercises as practice for replacing negative thoughts with more positive dialogue.

Destructive and Constructive Thinking Patterns

Choose the typical thought you would say to yourself for each event described (D-destructive; C-constructive).

Event	Internal Dialogue Choice
1. I separated from my spouse, whom I had been with for fifteen years.	D: He/she was unfair and I am going to get back at them. C: I had a long relationship, and now I need to rediscover it or find another one.

2. I was laid off from my job after one year.

D: This was unfair because I was new and didn't get a chance.

C: At least they saw my worth in hiring me, and others will too.

3. I failed an important test, and the reaction of my family was not supportive.

D: Those stupid slugs. All they care about regarding my success is their esteem with others.

C: They were probably uncomfortable with me, so I need to tell them.

4. I was turned down for a date.

D: I must not be as good as I thought, and might be lucky to find someone else.

C: The right person has not surfaced yet.

5. I see an old friend who seems to avoid or ignore me.

D: I am embarrassed because he or she does not want to associate with me.

C: He or she has their mind on something else, something that could be serious to them.

6. My job application was just turned down.

D: They didn't like me because they were stupid and I was different.

C: This was not the right place for me, and I learned something useful for the next time.

7. My friend got into a close relationship with a person I wanted to meet.

D: My friend probably sabotaged me, maybe told them something bad about me.

C: At least I know there are people out there for people like him/her and we can all be friends.

8. I could not buy a new car because the bank turned my loan down based on my salary.

D: The world is unfair and I feel resentful and angry.

C: It is good to have priorities for your wants because they tell you who you are.

9. I spend time in the home all day because I am depressed.

D: There is no use going out, so I am going to just try to nurture myself with food or drink.
C: I want to study up on my skills and consider the potential new opportunities to find joy out there.

10. My birthday was yesterday.

D: I am getting older and running out of luck.
C: I am gaining experience and understanding better what I want to do in my life.

Choose the most *constructive* thinking you could have as a reaction to each event or situation:

11. I was one of the final two candidates for a great job, but I didn't get it.

A. Those people deliberately wasted my time.
B. They never told me how I was doing in comparison to the other person.
C. I must be good to have gotten that far . . . I'll find out why I didn't get to the finish line and learn from it for the next opportunity.

12. I worked hard to make a good grade and then I found out that my grade was not high.

A. That dumb teacher just didn't tell me the right things to study.
B. I will call back and meet with the teacher to find out exactly what the reasons were. It will give me another chance to make a better grade.
C. I guess the teacher just didn't like me.

13. I'm a great candidate for a job in the company I work for. I have asked about it, but they haven't called me.

A. I will pick up the phone, find who is the hiring authority, call him, and discuss what I could do to be more valuable for the company.
B. Can't those people read a résumé and see that I am perfect? They are too dumb for my time.
C. Maybe I should e-mail my résumé to another company and quit this one.

14. One of my friends just got into a great college, and my first-choice school rejected me.

A. I am worth little, and I have been fooling everyone.
B. I should investigate how other individuals have been successful and compare myself to them.
C. I need to assess myself as to my own positive features and choose goals that would help me feel that I have power to be successful for myself.

15. I've had three job interviews this month, and none of the prospective employers have called.

A. I must not be explaining very clearly the benefits of hiring me.
B. They just aren't asking me the right questions.
C. They aren't smart enough to understand my value.

16. I am afraid to make decisions because I know that I will probably make a mistake.

A. I really get upset when everyone disagrees or criticizes me.
B. I know that I cannot make everyone happy and agree with me. I will have to make a decision based on my own needs instead of someone else's.

C. I will try to figure out what everyone thinks before I make a decision based on the consensus.

17. I should probably leave my abusive spouse, but I believe that he/she really loves me and needs me to take care of him/her.

A. I probably provoke my spouse's anger, so it is my fault he/she acts that way toward me.
B. When you are as weak as I am you just have to take what you in get life.
C. I need to actively pursue what is best for me and in my best interests.

18. I believe I have a limited intellect because I got bad grades in school.

A. I should assess my intellect based on more current tests that reflect my unique abilities. School performance is just one kind of intellectual ability.
B. My intelligence cannot grow since I have become an adult.
C. I never was good with numbers and that is what it takes to be smart.

19. I'm fifty-six and my life seems to be over as far as trying to achieve something or making any money.

A. Life opportunities dry up when you get old like me.
B. My brain can grow at any age and my opportunities can grow. My vast experience can be a great advantage.
C. My brain is dwindling down to where I can't remember anything and I can't do anything about it.

20. I was abused when I was a child and cannot trust people again.

A. Once you have a damaged mind it can never repair itself to being normal, like other people's.

B. I can make the decision to release the attitude that I am damaged and actively pursue a healthy goal in the future.

C. It is all my parents' fault that I am having a rough time in life now.

Fill in your own event and responses:

(Event)   D:

                                 C:

(Event)   D:

                                 C:

Scoring:

The most constructive responses for items 11–20 are below:

Item 11	C	Item 16	B
Item 12	B	Item 17	C
Item 13	A	Item 18	A
Item 14	C	Item 19	B
Item 15	A	Item 20	B

If you missed more than two, it would be important for you to reevaluate what you are saying to yourself and how you are creating your own negative thinking. When you let things that happen to you trigger negative and self-destructive behavior, you lose the opportunity to learn and move forward. To grow and achieve better outcomes, you need to take responsibility for your responses to negative events in your life. By using your intellect and your power to choose how you respond, you turn them into positive experiences.

CONCLUDING COMMENTS ON RIGHT THINKING

It is not uncommon for graduate school programs to require a course in critical thinking as part of their curriculum because students need to fully optimize their thinking abilities. The same principle holds true for all of us. You can make better choices for your life when you can do so without the burden of negative self-talk and destructive internal dialogue. These factors are much more critical than an IQ score because you cannot apply your knowledge and creativity when you are operating under self-imposed false assumptions.

The human brain is a marvel of discovery that we have yet to fully understand. This six-pound mechanism has helped us enjoy the abundance of life, yet it can also serve to imprison us in bonds of suffering and despair. The amazing fact is that we have a choice, but it takes strength and encouragement to take that much power into our own hands. Developing the wisdom and experience to manage such a powerful resource is the fundamental quest of life.

Ten

INTERPERSONAL EMPOWERMENT

At the age of thirteen, Oliver experienced the typical highs and lows of adolescence. The high point was being "claimed" by the cutest girl in his class. The low point was being targeted for harassment by the class bully, Dwayne.

Oliver was no fool. He quickly figured out that the high point and the low point were related. Dwayne had never messed with him until the cute girl singled out Oliver for her affections.

Dwayne was the leader of a small group of boys who terrorized the playground. They weren't that much bigger, they just had more attitude and they hunted in a pack. Oliver had seen Dwayne in action with other kids. The bully set up his victims by claiming they'd "dissed" him in some way. Most would deny the allegation, but Dwayne would harass them until some favor was extracted.

Research on bullies has found that their typical motivation is a lack of self-esteem. Physical dominance is a compensation for that. Oliver could see that he was on Dwayne's radar and he wasn't looking forward to the attention. The bully's pack liked to haze Dwayne's targets and make them the butt of their jokes. Whether it's schoolboys or wolves in the wild, this is typical of pack psychology. The alpha male establishes his supremacy, and the others curtail their aggressiveness, unless in service to the alpha male, toward others. They become less competitive and demonstrate fewer creative behaviors, even when the bully is not present.

Oliver was no social scientist or psychologist, but he knew bullies could make his life miserable for the entire school year. And he had his image with a cute girlfriend to worry about. He felt he had his own reputation to uphold. So he asked his father how to handle Dwayne.

In surveys of parents and how they talk to their children about bullies, the findings are revealing. Ninety-nine percent of mothers will tell their child to walk or run away because physical injury is worse than shame and "violence never resolves anything."

Ninety percent of fathers, who have more experience in this issue, advise their children to stick up for themselves. They note that self-esteem is more important than a bloody nose over the long term. Oliver's father thought of an alternative: "If you can't talk your way out of this, then you have the two obvious choices—fight or flight."

Oliver asked his dad to help him come up with a plan of attack. They discussed three options:

1. He could try psychology and figure out why Dwayne was a bully and help him work on his esteem issues.

2. He could humor Dwayne and pretend to be terrified to disarm him.

3. He could find a way to make friends with the bully.

I had to hand it to Oliver, the kid had moxie. As it turned out, he did all three. When Dwayne and his pack came calling in the middle of the school year, in front of the entire student body, Oliver was ready for them.

"I hear you've been calling me names behind my back, and I'm gonna put a stop to that crap," Dwayne said, spitting into Oliver's face.

"Oh yeah, what did you hear? Why would I say anything about you?" responded Oliver.

This threw Dwayne off stride. He'd never had to provide evidence before.

"Let's just say that I don't like you and your mouth needs to be shut up," Dwayne said lamely.

Then Oliver turned up the charm.

"Dwayne, you are obviously a smart guy. I hear you have talent too, with the harmonica. And I know you get all the girls. So I can't figure out why you'd want to pick a fight with a guy like me. But since you want to fight, why don't we go down to the boxing gym where we can really do it right. You don't need to make up a reason to fight there. Of course, if you are just having a bad day and decided to pick on me because I'm standing here, we can always reschedule the fight at your convenience."

Now Dwayne was really baffled. Oliver was complimenting him and challenging him at the same time. Dwayne was losing his advantage and he knew it, but he couldn't figure out how to shake this guy's confidence.

Finally he replied: "Yeah, let's go to the gym later so I can beat your brains out."

And that was the end of it. Without throwing a punch, Oliver knocked all of the fight out of Dwayne. As it turned out, the two of them did box each other as part of a recreation program a few months later. Oliver had gained just enough self-confidence from their earlier encounter that he didn't back down. That threw Dwayne off even more. Like most bullies, he wasn't nearly as tough as he acted.

Their bout ended in a draw with no blood drawn. But the real winner was Oliver, who discovered inner strength and resources that he built upon in the years that followed. Stepping up to the bully's challenge triggered a big leap in his emotional development. He began to compete with confidence first in spelling bees, then in arithmetic races, and later in team sports.

By the time I met Oliver, he was sixteen. He told me the story of his confrontation with Dwayne three years earlier and he explained the impact it had on his life. Oliver learned that he could take command of a situation by using his wits and his courage. His self-confidence enabled him to reach out to others so that he became a leader and an excellent team player with strong problem-solving skills. His story is a great example of the power of interpersonal dynamics. Through sheer strength of personality and will, Oliver not only defeated a bully, he set his life on a positive direction.

UNDERLYING INTERPERSONAL POWER

Human beings affect one another in exhilarating, terrible, and ecstatic ways. We are born into a world of relationships. We are initially defined by our membership in a community or family. Each person quickly learns what qualities are valued within a culture. The first requirement is to conform to established norms. This may come at the price of our individuality, but the price is higher if we are exiled. The basic punishment for crimes against a culture is exile. Rejection is one of the most feared human experiences.

Most people can conform to a culture by following its social rules, speaking its language, and obeying its laws. If taught from birth, many of these values are followed at an unconscious level. They become ingrained in our character.

However, even imagined transgression of these imbedded concepts can lead to severe conflicts within ourselves, requiring social rituals for forgiveness, even if no explicit harm is done. Most cultures, for example, have sanctions against incest. Freud reported that women suffered severe hysteria when they imagined having sexual relationships with their fathers, making dreams and urges as sinful as actual behavior.

Groups have great power over their members' perceptions and judgment. One of the classic studies in this regard was conducted by Solomon Asch. The study asked subjects to assess which line in box B was most similar to the one displayed in box A, like the one below:

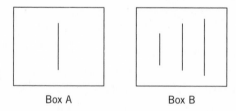

Box A   Box B

Eighteen comparisons were displayed with obvious answers. The test subject was asked to offer answers along with other people in a group. But the other people were conspirators and answered the questions in predesigned ways. They answered the first six frames correctly and the last twelve incorrectly.

The results of the study showed that subjects gave the socially desired wrong answers 70 percent of the time, even though they knew they were giving incorrect answers. In further investigations, the tendency to purposely give the socially accepted answer was compared and correlated with the number of the incorrect majority. The number of influential members required to change a person's responses dramatically increased from one, reaching a critical level with four people, and maxing out at seven (see below).

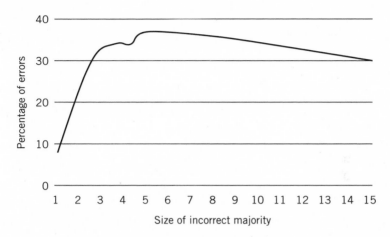

The fact that social pressure is so strong is not surprising. It's become a major factor in both advertising and politics. No one should passively give in to social pressure, but everyone should understand how it works and its potent influence. Friends, family, classmates, teammates, and other human beings influence us all. Yet we also possess an innate desire to form our own opinions and to act on our own thoughts and desires. It is natural to be swayed by social pressure, but it is also natural to want to *differentiate* oneself. We all experience the occasional conflict between the instinctual need for acceptance and protection versus our need to express our independence and individuality.

Most of this book has to do with the emergence of your authentic self and how to focus and maximize your inner strengths. But I would be limiting your powers if I did not address the fact that there is strength in numbers as well. The development of your special talents is extremely important, but the equation is not complete without tapping all the available sources of power around you.

My friend Dr. Phil McGraw is an enormously talented man, and there is no question that his success as the "Nation's Shrink" is attributable to his wisdom and intellect. However, he is also a master of tapping into the enormous power of society as a whole. His talent for organizing

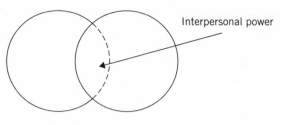

Interpersonal power

Your social power

three multimillion-dollar enterprises employing hundreds of people also says something about his power to pull together special individuals and their talents for a common purpose.

How do you develop the talents and abilities to use your social powers to the fullest? How do you step into a leadership role in your community and develop resources? How do you become a leader within a collective of individuals and get them to accomplish goals that have benefit for everyone? Interpersonal power is awesome.

ASSESSMENT OF SOCIAL STRENGTH

I have devised a short questionnaire to help you assess whether or not you have social skills and resources. Please answer the following descriptions in terms of how True (T), Sometimes True (ST), Rarely True (RT), or Never True (NT) they are for you.

1. I naturally assume a role of leadership in a group.

   T   ST   RT   NT

2. I find it hard to combat group decisions, even when I know that I am right.

   T   ST   RT   NT

3. I enjoy bringing order to confusing and chaotic social situations with my ability to handle people.

   T   ST   RT   NT

4. I am afraid of standing up and speaking to a group of people, especially if I feel that they don't like me.

    T   ST   RT   NT

5. I am a good listener.

    T   ST   RT   NT

6. I find it difficult to ask people, especially my friends, to help me when I am overwhelmed with responsibilities.

    T   ST   RT   NT

7. I like to compete with others because it helps develop my skills and abilities, even if I lose.

    T   ST   RT   NT

8. I fear embarrassment and ridicule most of all.

    T   ST   RT   NT

9. I know how to organize people to accomplish goals and feel a sense of accomplishment in doing so.

    T   ST   RT   NT

10. I don't know how to deal with someone who is angry with me or even with someone different from me.

    T   ST   RT   NT

11. I can handle most group situations to my advantage, probably better than anyone else.

    T   ST   RT   NT

12. I want to escape the situation when someone becomes angry and uncooperative.

    T   ST   RT   NT

13. I can create a helping and caring relationship with most anyone, even when they are hostile.

    T   ST   RT   NT

14. I am afraid of bullies because I may have to make a decision to defend myself.

    T   ST   RT   NT

Scoring:

For the odd-numbered items (1, 3, 5, 7, 9, 11, 13), credit each rating of True (T) with a value of 3, each rating of Sometimes True (ST) with a value of 2, and each rating of Rarely True (RT) with a value of 1. Total that subset for a score in the range of 0 to 21 (subtest odd = _____). For the even-numbered items (2, 4, 6, 8, 10, 12, 14), credit each rating of True (T) with a value of 3, each rating of Sometimes True (ST) with a value of 2, and the rating of Rarely True (RT) with a value of 1. Total these items for a subset score in the range of 0 to 21 (subtest even=_____). Subtract subtest even from subtest odd (or the other way around, depending on which has the greater value), for a total score in the range from –21 to +21.

    For example, assume that the subtest even items total was 12 and the subtest odd was 15, your total score would be 15 – 12=3. If your subtest even items total was 15, and your odd-numbers total was 12, your total score would be 15 – 12=3.

    Compare your total scores to the interpretations below:

Score	Interpretation
+ 11 to + 21	You have good skills and confidence to mobilize the social forces to empower you toward your goals.

+5 to +10	You have confidence in dealing with social forces to help you; however, these skills appear to be specific to familiar circumstances.
−5 to +4	You are ambivalent as to your skills to mobilize social forces around you, depending on the extent to which you perceive the situation as challenging to your capacities.
−10 to −6	You lack the confidence to confront negative social forces that are oppositional to your power. The following pages should be very important to your success.
−11 to −21	You are a victim of the social forces that confront you and you lack the abilities to utilize them for your individual needs. The following pages are required reading for you in order to stop relinquishing your power to these forces and to take charge of them for your own purposes.

AVOIDING THE HOOK IN NURTURING ONE'S POWER

In a recent conversation with Phil Davis, developer of *Decisions: The Drug Prevention Game,* we were discussing the power of peer pressure and a person's decision to use drugs as a conforming behavior. The analogy of the fish story came up. The story starts with a question: Why do fish want to eat the worm dangling at the end of a hook? The answer is simply that the fish is hungry and his survival is based on the intake of food. Fish cannot resist the food. It is a basic need. A fish does have the capacity to know how to avoid the hook but his destiny is sealed once he makes the choice to go for the worm.

Group affiliation is also a basic need. Like the hook in the worm, there are dangers inherent in always trying to fulfill that need. But unlike the fish, we can make choices based on knowledge and experience. Sometimes we may decide that the costs of a particular group affiliation are too great and we have to find other outlets for social interaction.

Okay, fishies. It's time to learn the most dangerous types of "hooks" hanging out there in the people pond. There are four big ones to avoid.

We'll call them the Rescuer, the Controller, the Pity Demon, and the Status Police.

The Rescuer tries to protect you from threats or disappointment at all costs, and in doing so, robs you of your own powers of self-determination. This person is mostly afraid that he or she will never be needed by you or anyone else. The Rescuer has to show how indispensable he is. The classic case is the parent who maintains a permanent wall around her child, never allowing the child to hurt herself or to feel discomfort. The real message to the child is, "You are incapable of dealing with the world and its dangers, therefore I must protect you." This example is not an indictment of parental concerns because this same relationship can exist between friends and marriage partners. The hook is that you may give up your power and miss out on critical opportunities.

The Controller is generally a masterful manipulator who will do anything to keep you from exercising your own power. Physical violence is not out of the question for this often abusive personality type. The Controller's identity relies on being right and being in control. Anyone who gets in the way of the Controller's objectives faces punishment or exile. He will hook you by offering to be of assistance, but you'll soon find yourself being dragged in all directions against your will. Being a part of a powerful social group can be alluring, but when the Controller is in charge—and one usually is—being part of the "in" crowd comes at a heavy toll.

The Pity Demon oozes empathy and hooks its "fish" by reinforcing their view of themselves as victims. If you are wallowing in being wronged, the Pity Demon will join you in the muck. You will never again have to go solo at the pity party. Whatever injustice or conspiracy has occurred, whoever has done you a bad turn will be vilified, cursed, and condemned by the Pity Demon. Ain't it a shame? Life sucks, then you die! Let's have another shot of Jack Daniel's!

The lure cast by the Pity Demon is aimed at your need for understanding and companionship and reinforcement. But the line is that there is no hope and that's the sinker too! To lose hope is the most disabling thing of all. You can lose your arms and your legs and still lead a wonderful life. But if you lose hope, you have no purpose. The Pity Demon does not want you to have hope because his power lies in your helplessness.

The Status Police are always on guard to protect their position. They'll pull out the big guns if they see you becoming stronger, skinnier, healthier, happier, richer, or more influential than they are. This is jealousy and envy taken to the tenth power. They hook you by inviting you into their circle, but if you show any signs of growing beyond its borders, they will cut you off at the knees.

These people are always on the alert for ways to keep you in check, hold you back, and tear you down to further their own agendas. You can pretty much rest assured that the Status Police will never be happy for your success. They will never celebrate your victories or happiness with sincerity. I had the privilege of joining the faculty at my alma mater. Joining your former teachers on the faculty can be a good thing, and it can also be a bad thing, depending on how many Status Police are lurking in the lounge. I taught for five years in this position and spent a good deal of time converting my relationship with each person from that of a student to that of a peer. I worked hard, published more than anyone, received more grants, and served beyond the call of duty. We were comfortable with each other and I felt a kinship. Yet I noticed that whenever it appeared that I might be rising above my peers in status, financial rewards, or accomplishment, the kinship became strained.

These toxic types toss out the lures of inclusion and belonging and friendship but they'll yank it back anytime you try to wiggle free of their control. The most vehement will do whatever it takes to remain in power. This might include offering you drugs, sex, money, status— whatever might tempt you to sign over your freedom to them. Street gangs are full of folks like this, but so are country clubs, corporations, academic departments, and athletic clubs. It is up to you to recognize when they are baiting the hook.

DEFINING YOUR OWN SOCIAL POWER

You will have a better chance of dodging toxic control freaks in social settings if you define what goes into a more positive and empowering relationship. Don't make the mistake of thinking that everyone should always be on your side and fully supportive. That is not very realistic anyway. And most of us benefit from healthy competition as well as cooperative and mutually supportive relationships.

Competition can be a very empowering dynamic. That's good, since someone is always out there competing against you for work, love, or money. You can't escape that, so you might as well embrace it. The competitive relationship is as natural as any other. But there are rules for keeping it healthy, and there are consequences for breaking those rules. So the first rule is that there are rules.

The second rule is that there will be a winner and a loser for every event. Just recognizing that will help keep things on a good level. Too many competitors pin their whole sense of identity on the outcome of each event. When competition becomes synonymous with increasing power over someone else instead of empowering oneself, things turn ugly in a hurry. Lance Armstrong's mother offered her thoughts on this. When Lance first began to bicycle race competitively, he showed very little indication that he would one day be a global phenomenon. But his mother encouraged him to focus on improving his times instead of racing to beat more accomplished bicyclists. She told him to make each race a challenge within himself. With that focus, Armstrong competed against the clock instead of against his fellow racers, and he beat the clock like no one has ever beat it before!

Competitive relationships remain healthy when you see your competitors as enablers rather than enemies. They enable you to test yourself against the best. They help you push yourself. They give you inspiration. They help you focus. Remember, you don't compete to keep from losing, you compete to win. The primary difference between a champion and a loser is that focus. Bart Starr, quarterback of the first Super Bowl champion Green Bay Packers, said: "We never lost a game. We just ran out of time before we scored more points. In our minds we could always win."

Regardless of the form of competition, it is wise to choose a competitor who pushes you to develop your talents to the fullest and to hone your skills. If you run out of time and you lose, look to see whether or not you still improved your performance so that you keep getting better and better. Embrace the competition for what you can gain from the experience of testing yourself with the best. I was a pretty good tennis player in college, but I knew I could only get better if I played against the best. I will admit that I "ran out of time" more often than not, but I enjoyed testing myself against those with skills I admired. I never wanted to play a less talented player just so I could win. There was no honor in that.

Great competitive relationships are sources of energy for both combatants. Muhammad Ali was the underdog when he met George Foreman for the World Heavyweight Championship the first time. Ali was uncharacteristically passive during the first three rounds. He allowed George Foreman to hit him repeatedly. But later in the match, Ali stepped up, took control and won. This boxing genius later explained that in the early rounds, he imagined himself absorbing his opponent's energy every time the powerful Foreman hit him. So as the fight progressed, Ali thought of himself as growing stronger and stronger while Foreman got weaker. You and I might not want to take that kind of beating, but Ali knew what he was doing. I often use his image of absorbing strength from an opponent and it works—as long as it doesn't involve letting the other guy use me as a punching bag.

In competitive relationships, you seek to develop your talents and skills to their highest levels. In cooperative relationships, you look to melding your talents and skills with others' so that your combined efforts can accomplish more than might be done individually.

Cooperation also calls for a thoughtful approach to leadership. Different types of leadership are appropriate for different situations. Direct leadership is the kind practiced by master drill sergeants. Their command and control approach is most effective—and most necessary—in the crisis and chaos of a battlefield when success depends on a clearly defined chain of command and unquestioning compliance with orders. Winston Churchill is often regarded as having enormous strength and wisdom in leadership, yet he failed miserably until the crisis of World War II afforded him the opportunity. These occasions call for confident direction and guidance.

Direct or chain-of-command leadership is not as effective outside of life-and-death situations. Sports coaches generally practice a slightly more relaxed form—but not always. These leaders motivate not from the top down, usually, but by generating power within the group. By creating a collective goal in which everyone has a stake, the leader can empower the entire team.

A third kind of leadership is subtle yet provocative. It is called the "conscience-driven" approach. This type of leader finds a cause or need that is greater than the individual needs of his followers. Often, this is a "noble" cause for social justice, charity, or dire need. Mother Teresa was a fragile, impoverished woman yet she rose to a position of international leadership by leading a global effort to help the neediest of the needy.

SOCIAL POWER SKILLS

What does it take to be a leader? What skills do you need? Are there "born leaders" or can anyone step up? Is life really a choice between leading, following, and getting out of the way? There are people who seem to have natural leadership abilities, but others can learn to lead by understanding the dynamics and the traits that inspire people to follow and comply. After all, you can't be a leader if no one is willing to listen to your directions.

I once served as director of research for the University of Arkansas Rehabilitation Research and Training Center. There we studied constructive interpersonal power between psychotherapists and their clients. We learned that the most productive psychotherapists empowered their clients rather than wielding power over them.

The three most important dimensions of their leadership involved:

1. Empathy

2. Positive regard and caring

3. Sincerity

These three attributes created the basis for positive decision making, self-awareness, and confidence, regardless of how much education, prestige, or training the therapists had. The implication was that while training and education are important, the real secret to being an effective therapist is to be a good leader. Let's look at each of those attributes in more depth.

Empathy

Understanding is a basic need. We all want our feelings and emotions to be validated by others. When others say they understand how we feel, it helps us clarify our perceptions of the world. Empathy is the expression of understanding without critical judgment or personalization.

This is empathy: "You lost twenty-five pounds? That's great! You should be very proud of yourself. What an accomplishment!"

This is not empathy: "You lost twenty-five pounds? Well, you really needed to lose at least that much, didn't you? I hope you aren't stopping there!"

Nor is this empathy: "You lost twenty-five pounds? I really need to lose some weight too. I was just thinking that I'd better stop eating doughnuts for breakfast and candy bars for lunch. Gosh, I could lose even more than twenty-five pounds if I did that!"

Empathy is the expressed understanding of someone else's unique experience. It is not about shared feelings or experiences. The power of true empathy cannot be overestimated. It requires that you invest in someone else and that you listen so that you truly understand them, but the rewards can be significant. When people feel that they are heard and valued, they offer their trust. There is no greater or more precious gift.

Empathy skills are valuable across the board of human interactions. The more empathy you show in a sales relationship, the higher the probability that you will seal the deal. The more understanding you are to your spouse or lover, the deeper your relationship will become. The more empathic you are to your child, the better behaved they will be. Empathy is a powerful social tool because it pays off in trust, and trust is a universal currency that pays huge dividends.

By listening to the emotions of others you can understand their sensitivities and biases and their sources of support, but most of all you know their needs. You know because they will tell you, if you listen intently and hear what they are really saying. Having this knowledge gives you the power of understanding the deepest secrets that silently shape their worlds.

Positive Regard and Caring

Everyone wants to be cared for and held in positive regard. Yet how this is translated can have problematic interpretations. From the time we are infants we want to be held and cuddled. The nature of our nurturance can be the basis of life itself. Babies who are not cared for in this way have a higher incidence of disease and death than those who receive a minimum of touching and stroking. The research on "therapeutic touch" validates that energy extended through touching does have healing impact on wounds and also emotional conditions.

Yet there are widely different views of what constitutes "caring." Italians often hug and yell at each other as a form of positive regard. Some tribes of Native Americans express caring through intimate conversation and the exchange of gifts. Many cultures offer ways of expressing care through "meta-communication" that is not verbalized. It comes in the form of touching, facial expressions, acts of kindness, and unconditional support. In professional therapy, patients may be confused by caring behaviors and misinterpret them as sexual in nature. This creates nothing but problems, so specific boundaries may have to be formally expressed. The therapist always needs to let the patient know that security and safety are primary concerns.

Displays of caring and positive regard are powerful social tools. My own studies have found that up to 75 percent of people respond more to nonverbal expressions of caring over verbal. I worked with Dr. Phil when he was directing Courtroom Science, Inc., his forensic consulting firm. We helped evaluate jury decisions and expert credibility for trials. We found that the most critical elements a juror uses in measuring the believability of a witness's testimony are the witness's appearance and mannerisms. If the witness spoke in a very strained, nervous tone, the jury grew skeptical. If the witness appeared confident and looked at the jurors, they trusted the testimony more.

The same basic rules can be applied to building trust in social settings. These are critical meta-communication factors to consider when you want to build trust and influence:

- *Touch*—The tactile impact of a soft supportive touch carries enormous messages of trust and commitment.

- *Voice quality*—Softer tones create more need for attention than harsh tones, even though harsh tones do command a focus. Confidence is also perceived in a person who has a louder quality (not shouting, but if you want your point to be heard you need to raise your voice specifically to emphasize your issue).

- *Solid handshake*—Many people judge the sincerity of a person by their handshake. Be firm and confident to emphasize your persuasive abilities.

- *Eye contact*—The stronger the visual connection, the closer the bond between two people interacting.

- *Facial gestures*—The more affirmative your face is, the more a person will want to make an emotional connection. Using various facial gestures, such as smiling appropriately, nodding (as if understanding), and showing approval to ideas are all good. Picking your nose and yawning are really bad ideas.

- *Body language*—The more you "mirror" the posture of the person you are with, the stronger the connection.

- *Hand gestures*—The more you use your hands to denote a positive relationship, the better. Togetherness and agreement are communicated by pointing at the other person and then back to yourself repeatedly.

Sincerity

No one wants to be taken as a fool. People want respect. They want to deal with others who are honest and have integrity. To communicate sincerity, you must articulate your feelings and then "walk the talk." Sincerity is imparted through the expression of your feelings, not your opinions about another person.

To say "That person is a liar" only reflects an opinion, not a fact. It certainly does not relate to your feelings. A more correct, genuine statement would be, "I have been hurt by that person because he has appeared to lie to me, ruining my trust in him." This statement specifies that you are speaking from your own perspective and your personal reaction. The person may or may not have lied, but your sincere perception was that you misplaced your trust and paid a price.

People often ask me what to do in specific situations, such as dealing with an angry boss or unwanted relationships. I express sympathy but I don't generally offer my opinion because I don't have a clear picture of the situation—and I don't want someone else to have to deal with the consequences if my uninformed opinion is wrong.

Feedback to a person can also be handled through genuine sincerity, but feedback is not the same as criticism. Sincerity is based on your own feelings and reactions, not a personal judgment. If you and your spouse have a disagreement and your spouse says something that scares you, a critical response would be: "You are becoming a mean, selfish person." But a sincere response would be: "I am becoming afraid of you because you are raising your voice and I am assuming you are getting angry with me."

Sincerity does not create distance. It should bring you closer.

CHOOSING YOUR TEAM

The people you select for your "team" are critical to your success socially. As with any team, you need to find those people who support your goals and want you to succeed. These goals and successes include survival of serious disease and challenging events, business and economic endeavors, relationship conflicts like marriages and divorces, and all other life lessons we have to learn from in order to accomplish our destinies.

When you build your social power team, you'll need some specialty players with certain areas of expertise to help you meet the challenges you will surely encounter. Those special people include a mentor, a partner, a true believer, and a judge.

The Mentor

A mentor is that person who has expertise in your field and can help you through the challenges based on experience. If you are battling a physical problem, you might find a doctor or specialist who can explain the issues that confront you and what options you need to clarify. Although this can be your own doctor or health care professional engaged in your care, I would prefer that it be a person who can help you understand what your health professional tells you but in a more comforting environment than a doctor's office.

I had a heart attack in 1995 while in California. Luckily there was no permanent damage. I had a great doctor, Dr. John Schroeder of Stanford

Medical School. He was patient and direct with me, but I needed my own mentor and found one in Dr. Larry Dossey, who could explain the medical details in my language. I could then approach my medical team with more power and confidence. I designed a powerful healing program and refused to be a victim of the medical system.

We cannot know everything. An authority figure can be intimidating. You may feel powerless in the face of someone with more training and experience. So, you should feel free to bring in a trusted authority of your own to serve your needs. My personal response to facing challenges that intimidate me is to bring in the "big dogs." I'm perfectly willing to call a law school dean, a mayor, or a senator if I feel the need for a social power player.

The Partner

Your partner is your mate in your boat. You count on your partner as a sounding board to provide support and reassurance. Loyalty and commitment are also provided by partners. You need a friend who will be with you, right or wrong, through the end. He or she does not have to be smart or wise, clever or cute, or even nice. What you need on your team for social power is a trusting relationship.

The partner is more of a comforting presence than a hands-on person. Often, your relationship is built upon unconditional love, the sort that can be expected from a parent or grandparent. Mothers are great models for the silent, loving partner whose primary mission is to be a presence for your life.

The True Believer

The true believer is a person who has no objective sense of whether you are right or wrong, but will always serve as your cheerleader. The true believer sees the good things in life, and focuses on encouragement. They have to have reliable information in order to be credible cheerleaders, but that information needs to be on the positive side.

I remember one day I was called to the principal's office in high school for something I did wrong. I do not remember the offense, but it was probably because I was holding hands with my girlfriend, Nell, which was the major transgression known as ODA (Obvious Display of Affection). My aunt Sishoney was in the building—she was a librarian in the school system—and saw me waiting. She immediately came through the door and asked what I was doing there. I explained the ODA rap. She went directly to the principal's office and said, "Whatever he did, he didn't do it. I am here to protect him." The door was immediately closed to further discussion and ten minutes later I was told to return to my class.

Obviously my aunt had no idea what I had done, but she didn't care. She was on my team for better or worse. She was a true believer then and still is today. Talk about social power.

You need a true believer to champion your cause. To earn this sort of loyalty and support, you have to demonstrate integrity and strong principles as well as unbridled commitment to a purpose greater than your own personal needs.

The Judge

The judge is that person who serves as an objective observer. You don't seek assurance or advice from this person, but you can count on the judge to say things straight without worrying about your reactions or even dismissal. The judge can give you feedback in an objective way. This is the person who will tell you what you need to hear rather than what you want to hear. That person knows the world as it is and not what you want it to be.

OVERVIEW

You are born into a world with adults who initially define who you are and have total power over you. The need for acceptance and support never goes away because we are interdependent. To attempt to avoid those forces would be to diminish ourselves. "No man is an island" has many true implications for the strong interconnections among all beings on this earth.

The question is not whether this power exists, but whether you are prepared to harness it. Few of us are taught how to use social power. Some people use this power for constructive and some for destructive ends. Hitler was certainly a powerful leader, but was undone by his evil goals. Gandhi and Martin Luther King, Jr., on the other hand, had social power that they used for our benefit.

The skills for managing social power described in this chapter offer you many ways to empower yourself to great heights. You must have constructive goals with appropriate motivation. Social power is like trying to tame a snake. It can be very powerful if used for the right purposes, but it can also turn around and bite you if you don't assess yourself and your intentions carefully.

Eleven

RAISING THE LIMITS OF YOUR CREATIVITY

Most people consider me a creative person. I write books and develop stories. I paint and sculpt gourds into pieces of art, and I have even sold some of my gourd art. I have designed dried flower arrangements that decorate many people's homes. I write poetry and a few songs, although most of them are pretty corny. I produce and sell drumming CDs, and I pass the time picking away at my bass guitar when I am not busy making a living.

The creative process fascinated me as a psychologist. I began studying it after I returned to graduate school with the intention of finishing a master's degree in mathematics. Contrary to what most people believe, graduate mathematics does not involve additional formulas and advanced skills in calculus or computer modeling. We leave that to the accounting and computer departments. Graduate mathematics is more of a study of the theory and nature of number systems. For example, most junior high school kids learn about prime numbers, those numbers that cannot be divided by any other number besides themselves and one, such as 2, 3, 7, 11, and so forth. The quest would be to find the largest prime number possible. I cannot see much direct application to anyone's life for these exercises, but these issues were exciting to me, nonetheless.

As my classes proceeded, it was clear to me that solutions to these problems would take more than what was available in class. In fact, one problem took an entire semester to formulate and solve. A master's thesis in mathematics is usually one problem with its entire proof of logic.

Many problems existed within a larger one and each step required broader concepts to solve. I was in over my head quickly. The problems were simply too large to be grasped totally and had to be broken down.

What I ultimately discovered about creative problem solving may sound like a child's game to you, but it was the following process that worked consistently for me: Before bedtime, I would study all the elements required to solve the problem. Next, I would formulate in my head my mission for the project or problem. Then I would ask God to help me solve it, and release it to Him and the Creator's calculator in the sky.

At precisely 5:00 A.M., I would wake up from a dream and I would have the solution! The hard part was getting out of bed to write it down, because I also found that if I did not immediately write it down, it would dissolve before my normal waking time.

Today I use the same method. In fact, this is the way I wrote this book, as well as every other book I've ever written. I study the mission of what subjects I want to discuss. I ask God to help me to make it clear and relevant to the reader, and I go to sleep. At 5:00 A.M. I awake, and I write it down.

You might legitimately ask who is the real author of my books. I remember sitting down and writing a short novella, called *The Cure,* about a wolf who gets cancer and searches for the meaning of this disease throughout the forest. He finds his own answer and he feels cured of his real question, which was his need for internal peace and self-acceptance. This book has meant so much to a huge number of people because of its subtle messages, but to tell the truth I barely remember creating that manuscript. I felt more like a scribe than an author in bringing that book into existence.

The process I describe is not unique to me. In fact, in multiple studies of creative people, this process has almost exactly the same steps. There are differences in the specifics, of course, and the challenges change according to each person's goals and needs, but this is the wonderment of how the mind takes us into realms we did not know existed. It separates us from every other creature on earth. It is the opposite of the brain's disciplined thinking focus. It is more of a *non-thinking* focus.

DISCOVERY AND CREATIVITY: HOW THE BRAIN WORKS

The workings of the brain in the creative process differ sharply depending on what kind of problem you are trying to solve. As you'll recall, we measure the electrical output of the brain in areas of the cortex into five basic ranges, shown below as a reminder:

Name	Range	Consciousness status
Delta	.5–4 Hz	Sleep
Theta	4–8 Hz	Hypnologic trance
Alpha	8–12 Hz	Relaxation
LoBeta	12–15 Hz	Focus
HiBeta	16-plus Hz	Confusion, lack of focus

When we focus on problems and use our brains to learn basic rational relationships and cogent associations, such as the logic of $3 \times 4 = 12$ or the memory of who discovered radium, our brain is normally in a state of LoBeta. It is transferring information from one area of the brain to another. In fact, the brain waves actually look like they have information in codes that resemble the shapes of the printed forms, such as letters of the alphabet or music notes.

By contrast, the low Alpha waves do not carry information because you are relaxed to the point of no longer learning. But while the LoBeta waves transfer information, the HiBeta wave form is too narrow to carry much data. The waves of each range are similar to voice patterns.

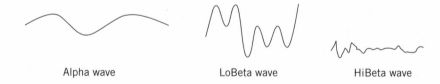

Alpha wave   LoBeta wave   HiBeta wave

When you enter a creative state, your brain basically switches from a LoBeta frequency to a Theta state. You actually stop focusing and release the brain to do the work itself in its own time. The frontal lobe, which normally manages the learning and executive functions for you to get through the day, stops its oversight and shuts down. However, the other lobes begin to light up more, especially the occipital lobe if you are using imagery, and the temporal lobes that relate to memory. For example, in your sleep, there is a stage five in which your whole brain goes into Delta state, but when you start dreaming and have REM sleep, the brain lobes begin firing off with high Alpha and LoBeta scenarios. These dreams contain those parts of the creative process that you will want to remember.

You might say that when I asked God to take over, I released my brain to do its thing. Then I could switch off my attention button. This is not a rejection of a theological explanation; there is an argument that our spirituality can rest in the body as well as in the universe.

The steps your brain takes are mysterious and they may never be completely comprehended. We do know that there are specific functions your brain performs when you ask a question. Two that appear to be instinctual are the *interpolation* and *extrapolation* functions.

The need to interpolate means the brain has the inherent instinct to make sense of the action or process between the beginning and ending of a story. Let's say I told you a short story about a little princess who was very lonely and wanted to live in a crystal mountain. If I suddenly jumped to a year later in the story and said that the princess was married to John and they were living in a crystal mountain, you would want to know how she found John, if she was still lonely, and how the heck do you live in a rock?

The psychological term for this innate need for completion of a perception is called a *gestalt,* which forms the concept for a therapy for discovering the total self referred to as Gestalt psychology. There is a natural tendency for the mind to complete the picture or concept from small bits into a whole concept.

Let me clarify this with a short exercise using some diagrams. We use unconscious methods of perceiving wholes with our need for closure and by choosing the simplest of whole perceptions. For example, in figure A on page 188, you would typically see two groups of three instead of six separate circles. In B, the similarity principle would predict that you would see two columns of X's and two columns of O's instead of four rows of XOXO's. The continuity principle would apply to figure C, where you would probably see the two components of the whole figure of the "X" made up of two lines instead of two V's. In figure D, your

mind would create a triangle or a square from the basic angles for closure, and your mind would prefer to see the three-dimensional box in
figure E rather than the two-dimensional hexagon—although both represent the same figure—because it is simpler.

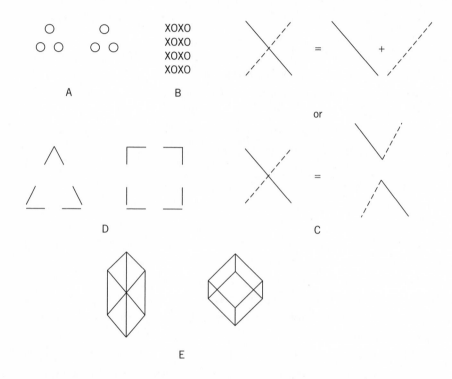

These neurological needs of the brain can easily be experienced with
the simple observation of seeing an airplane fly into a cloud. As you
track the airplane flying into and out of a cloud, you naturally assume
that there is no event between these two events. But if the plane comes
out at another place or disappears, we begin to get disturbed. The confusion creates the tension to force us to want to learn.

Extrapolation is that need for your brain to predict a certainty in the
future. Like interpolation, which tries to understand between two
times, extrapolation is the extension of events. For example, if you ob-
serve a sailboat traveling from the left of your vision to the right, your
brain will naturally predict that based on an estimate of movement it
should travel to the far right of your view at a certain pace. This is the

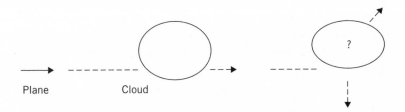

Plane   Cloud

basic function your brain serves as you ask it to make a choice to pass a car on a two-lane highway or hit a baseball coming at you. This is primarily an unconscious function your brain performs in order for you to live a predictable life.

I mention these two instinctive functions of interpolation and extrapolation because these are the questions for which the brain likes to create answers. These are the types of activities it does best by itself as a form of the creative process. It fills in the blanks naturally if you give it enough time to process the information you have built up. Ask it to explain or project the kind of image or statement you are trying to express. Ask it to find answers in the gaps of your knowledge. You don't have to train it to create some explanation or solution, but you may have trouble understanding the output because the brain doesn't use the English language. It uses symbols and these symbols have multiple meanings.

The reason we often do not understand our dreams is because these communications have multiple meanings. If I am seeking a solution to a physics problem during the day and that night I have a dream of snakes, I have to ask what the dream might mean in relation to my physics problem. I'm not hallucinating from venom when I say the two could well be related. James Watson, cowinner of the Nobel Prize, purportedly actually had a dream of two snakes in a circle one night, and within that dream, he found the answer to the long-sought structure of the DNA molecule.

We all have a certain level of creativity, but many people simply don't know how to tap into that part of the brain. Often, we fail to draw upon the brain's creative capabilities because we are afraid of the consequences to our social obligations and expectations. We distort our creativities because we are fixated on what we want to perceive and not what is presented to us. For example, if you ran an experiment on gravity and your experiment demonstrated that you can reverse the gravity pull on an apple if you pray over it, how many of you would be willing to report your findings to the prestigious schools of MIT or Harvard for fear of losing your credibility as a scientist? Your mind cancels out a lot of events because you are too afraid to even contemplate the consequences of your observations, either professionally or personally. You have constructed a worldview of how things are supposed to happen, and getting your mind around any event that does not fit within this will require a new approach.

ASSESSING YOUR CREATIVITY RESOURCES

This questionnaire will measure how well you access your brain's creativity centers. It is also a measurement of your skills in "turning on" your creative mental powers. Mark each description according to how much it is True (T), Sometimes True (ST), Rarely True (RT), or Never True (NT) of you on a typical day.

1. When I try to be creative I just think of stupid ideas, and nothing really works.

   T   ST   RT   NT

2. I am too old to become creative, too set in my ways.

   T   ST   RT   NT

3. Creativity is something people are born with, and I was not one of those people.

   T   ST   RT   NT

4. I never have any dreams.

   T   ST   RT   NT

5. I am a procrastinator. I keep putting off my creative activities, like art interests, and I just never get to them.

   T   ST   RT   NT

6. I never finish my projects once I start.

   T   ST   RT   NT

7. I always feel that the products of my creativity are never perfect enough, and I am embarrassed when they are not ready for someone else to see or hear them.

   T   ST   RT   NT

8. I am impatient and get discouraged easily when I do not get creative, useful ideas.

   T   ST   RT   NT

9. I feel that I am paralyzed and prevented from doing something, so I find other things to do.

   T   ST   RT   NT

10. I remember when my ideas flopped and I was not happy with being criticized.

    T   ST   RT   NT

11. I am my own worst critic.

    T   ST   RT   NT

12. I have a fear that someone else has already done what I create, and probably has done it better.

    T   ST   RT   NT

13. The reason I can't be creative is because someone else is always bugging me.

    T   ST   RT   NT

14. I am hopeless in creating solutions.

   T   ST   RT   NT

15. I feel overwhelmed when I am challenged and there is no direct
    direction someone has given me.

   T   ST   RT   NT

Scoring:

For each True (T) you checked, give a credit of 3, for each Sometimes
True (ST) give a credit of 2, and for each Rarely True (RT) give a credit
of 1. Total your credits for a score in the range from 0 to 45, and compare
them to the interpretations below:

Range	Interpretation
38–45	This score indicates that you have little confidence in your creativity and your ability to find new ways of living or alternative solutions to problems. It is also a sign of depression and lack of personal spiritual connections.
25–37	This score indicates a lack of the sort of creative skills necessary for making passionate and positive changes in your life. You may have a fear of change.
15–24	This score indicates a lack of confidence in other people to solve your problems. However, there are signs of appreciation for your own intuition and tentative trust in deeper unconscious resources.
9–14	This score indicates that you appreciate your creative powers and that you have developed some intuitive skills so that you can deal with change as a positive opportunity for growth.

0–8   This score indicates a mature confidence in your unconscious resources for harnessing creativity and following your passion. This score would indicate a person who has high levels of energy for pursuing goals with gusto and courage.

This test measures the barriers to your creativity because those are the primary issues for assessing the unconscious features that express your imagination. Creativity is a natural process, but we tend to mess it up with our fears and anxieties. Look at how you measure up, and if there are obstacles to tapping your full creativity, pledge to remove them so that you can experience the joys of your imagination.

WHY SEEK CREATIVITY?

Why should you be interested in creativity? Aren't there enough painting and art forms in Hobby Lobby or Michael's to satisfy any creative urge? Aren't there enough books written? But creativity is not just "making" crafts or art. It is a way of living. It is a tool for creating a future of your own design. There is no guide to steer you through the challenges that wait each day, week, month, or year. But those challenges will be there. And the more creativity you bring to each day, the greater the opportunities and the challenges that come with them. Creativity releases you from the shackles of fear and from stagnant concepts. It offers the freedom and joy that comes with the full expression of your talents and intellect. You can create a new life and new interpretations of your role. What will you become? With creativity, you are free to unleash your authentic self. But what does that mean when you wake up in the morning to go to work? Enlightenment is almost meaningless if it does not give you the power to make new choices about your life. It may mean a return to your home values. What sort of life would you want to create? How would you want to affect those around you?

These answers define the enrichment of your culture. By creating the visions of art, literature, imagery, teaching, etc., you are enriching the lives of others with a deeper reverence for spiritual growth. The role of creativity is to help all of us recognize that depth within us. Creative expression connects us all. Your road will be creative by the very definition of the process, and the more you travel on it the more enriching your life will become.

THE STEPS TOWARD CREATIVITY

There are four steps for tapping your creativity: immersion, incubation, symbolic formulation, and evaluation. Each step opens another gate into creativity. You may need to experiment to devise your own pathways, as this process is unique to every individual.

Immersion

The stage of immersion is the time in which you study everything you can about the creative challenges you are facing. If you want to paint something, study the kind of paint others use, the lines of perspective, etc. If you want to create a novel, read other novels, take a writing class, and so forth. If you want to invent a new mousetrap, study other mousetraps, the behavior of mice, etc. You must learn the basics to begin the process. Einstein didn't create the relativity theory by sitting around watching reruns on television.

In the immersion stage you learn which questions to ask. Creative activities such as writing poetry and song lyrics draw upon life experience, which is why the best work comes from the heart and touches others. If you have never been in love, don't write about it because you need to experience it to write about it. The best general advice is: *Write what you know.* Build your art around your experience and then let your imagination and creativity soar. I get peeved when some young kid tries to express pain or sorrow that he has no feeling for whatsoever. That is just empty air to me.

Don't be afraid to experiment with all sorts of creative material for inspiration. When I got stuck on mathematics problems, I often studied music theory to relax my mind. It always freed up my mind to find the math solutions. Fooling with my horses worked when I was seeking insight into psychotherapy issues. The brain loves data and will use different metaphors for creativity.

Incubation

The incubation period occurs when you switch your brain from LoBeta power to Theta power so the creative process kicks into gear. The trick is to allow this to happen without anxiety or fear. Anxiety is the enemy to creativity because it does not allow the brain to incubate in the hypnologic state where boundaries blur between our conventional thoughts. Fears distract the process completely. All creative people find the door into incubation. Albert Einstein used to play his violin to help him relax and "see" solutions to problems. Ernest Hemingway would write five hundred words on his novel and go down to his local tavern to get "relaxed."

The methods for switching the brain to "create" mode are numerous and interesting. Physical changes to the body can enhance the process. Here are a few common methods:

- Finding music from simple drumming to classical orchestras, dancing, chanting, and singing.

- Breathing specific patterns, such as the ones mentioned in chapter 2. Some people retreat for weeks for the purpose of focusing on their breathing experiences.

- Continuous dancing and movement, such as endless shuffling in a circle, swaying, rocking in a chair, rhythmic walking, Sufi dancing and twirling, kinesthetic movement representing the problems and questions.

- Incantations and prayer addressing a deity, source of knowledge, spirit of the hero, the "Buddha within," the "higher self," higher power, formal prayer, or imagery meditation, mantras, repetitions of statements such as "I am."

- Abstention from brain distractions in favor of celibacy, retreat from social contact, silence.

- Fasting from stimulating substances and activities, including caffeine, sugar, television, radio, or loud music.

- Stress induction that shifts the brain from ordinary consciousness, such as excessive physical ordeals: going for long periods while standing or dancing, sensory deprivation, pain induction as in sacrifice, fatigue, hunger, thirst.

- Alternative stimulations of the senses, such as smelling various flowers or herbs, burning incense.

- Environmental change, such as going to a sacred place (church, temple, etc.), the desert, ocean, mountains, a cave.

- Driving in solitude can be a very creative time. I get more things done in my car than in my office with creative steps and planning. Traffic jams are a blessing!

Dmitri Mendeleyev, a Russian, attended the First International Chemical Congress in Karlsruhe, Germany, in 1860 and was impressed by the discussion of methods for calculating atomic weight. On March 1, 1869, he fell into an exhausted state and woke up with the idea for the periodic table of elements, which is the groundwork for explaining the underlying pattern of nature.

Symbolic Formulation

The formulations or images that start emerging from the incubation stage are rarely understood immediately. The more complicated your questions and missions are, the more complicated the creativity process will be. Since the brain does not use language much, it uses symbols, making interpretation more difficult. Like dreams, sometimes the answers simply don't make sense.

As a longtime student of images and symbols, I have formulated seven basic sources of creative brain symbols that may be useful for your own interpretations. These have been used since ancient times for healing insight. Their applications can be seen in archeological ruins.

1. *Neurological hardwiring*—Every brain is hardwired with preset images, such as visual representations of spirals, lattices, webs, and basic geometric figures (circles, squares). It is not unusual

to have these figures crop up in your absentminded doodles. Spirals usually suggest deepening of self-reflection. The lattice usually refers to networking to other people or ideas, and the Web design is often interpreted as connections to a central figure or issue. Squares communicate the need for foundations. Circles commonly imply integration and harmony.

2. *Mind-body communication*—The body often sends messages that it needs help. They can be interpreted to help you gain insight into your creative processes. The image of the heart might symbolize your need for affection. Each bodily organ sends specific messages too. Your creative brain can read these and order the mind to generate concepts to represent possible behaviors that would serve as remedies. For example, motivation for a healthier and more creative new lifestyle might include the lattice of loved ones, the heart beating without the walls of fears, and the scene of running on glorious roadways as sources for contemplation in a joyous new stage in life. As you understand the complexities and have personal insights into what messages these symbols have for you, you can avoid more dangerous consequences. You may reach out to your love support, you may learn to release your fears, or you may embrace a new retirement phase that, if heeded, prevents the buildup of heart disease and related chronic stress conditions.

3. *Psychodynamics*—Many of the insights we derive from our creativity come from our internal dynamics. Creativity is often inspired by emotional turmoil or conflict. Passionate feelings drive deeper self-exploration. Broken hearts can inspire us to question the meaning of love or to express both pain and joy. The tragedy of *Romeo and Juliet* could only have been written by someone who experienced the sting and rapture of romantic love. The famous hymn "Amazing Grace" could only have been written by someone who had known what it was like to fall from grace and to bask in it too. The author of the hymn was John Newton, a slave trader who became an abolitionist. Newton was a man of paradoxes: for many years he earned his living from the slave trade, and yet he was for a short while enslaved himself, planting lime trees in

Sierra Leone. A horrific storm at sea in 1748 led Newton to his new life as a minister and antislavery activist. He recollected both his deliverance from the storm, and his life without God, in his most famous creation. Creativity is often forged through suffering or challenging times. These psychodynamics reveal themselves as art because they articulate the secrets within all of us. This is the stuff that differentiates creativity from technology.

4. *Nature*—Symbols of nature are prominent in our culture because our brains are part of nature's design. Natural elements such as wind, fire, and rain are prominent also in our dreams, another expression of our creativity. The horse, which is often a symbolic representation of strength, beauty, and freedom, appears widely, as does the eagle, another symbol of strength, freedom, and beauty, as well as wisdom and foresight. The interpretations of nature symbols are based on their function and personal association to one's values.

5. *Culture*—Just as natural symbols are determined by function and value to us, cultural images symbolize our beliefs. In some cultures the owl represents wisdom and mystery, in others it represents certain death. Money represents power for some people and in others it represents corruption. Creative people often use symbols to communicate messages subtly in their art. Leonardo da Vinci's paintings contained dozens of implicit cultural symbols that sent messages to his admirers and to his critics.

6. *Collective unconscious*—The "collective unconscious" is a psycho-logical term from the writings of Carl Jung, a master of creativity and an early colleague of Sigmund Freud. Jung was interested in the unconscious source from which creative symbology emerged. His view differed from Freud's psychoanalytic conclusion that all psychic energy, especially creativity, came from sexual energy. Jung's scientific analysis conceived through word association that a major source of creativity came from the collective thoughts and issues of our ancestors. His view was that creativity and wisdom are passed down to our brains as part of a legacy of consciousness to benefit each new generation with the wisdom of the previous generation. Because of that legacy being passed down we don't

have to keep learning the same truths over and over. The hope is that each new generation will have a better existence than the previous one because of lessons learned.

This is a comforting thought, much better than thinking that the wisdom of each lifetime is buried with the body that carried it. The relevance of this collective unconscious energy is that creativity seems to be its only avenue for expression. It is through the opening of our minds and the channels of our arts and works that these truths are given to us.

7. *Pure symbols*—The most controversial source of our creativity comes from a place beyond our knowledge. It has embedded within our unconscious the seeds of self-evolution. Many of these concepts were shared by Joseph Campbell in his description of the hero's journey and the role of the missionary as a messenger from the source we call God. This is the basic idea behind why individuals rise from their meager birthrights to have an amazing influence on world social evolution as part of their destinies, although they might have been the unlikely candidates. In spite of the fact that Edison, Einstein, Bill Gates, and a wide range of creative scientists took unconventional paths, they still achieved their grand destinies and were able to express their creativity. It makes you wonder how many creative souls never had the opportunity to share their gifts with us. Could it be that you have a seed of expression that requires nurturance, and that it can only receive it through your creativity? Perhaps this is a major reason for creativity, an avenue for the evolution of the human spirit, means for reaching the elevation of the angels and finding peace. Our creativity may be the blossoming of this potential.

Evaluation

Not all creative dreams or visions carry symbolic value. Some of it is just random stuff whipped up from the dregs of your unconscious. Bert was trying to create a song about the loss of a deep, loving relationship. He searched for the right lyrics that would express his feelings, but all he got for a week's efforts was a bunch of dreams about cleaning up his house and being back in his college days failing some stupid test. He was sure that these came from some issues he had about his life, but they were nothing he could use for his song. He meditated, listened to drumming, and fasted with no inspiration. He tried a lot of songs, but nothing hit his heart. Finally he took the time to go see a movie, *The Phantom of the Opera,* and that music opened the right door in his creative subconscious. He had to be in the right place mentally for the creative process to churn.

This process of opening the doors to creativity, and to finding poignant and imaginative words, can be tricky. It might take some tweaking, sifting, and listening to your heart. Some artists use trial and error methods, which is why you see them tearing up half-complete canvases or throwing pages of manuscript in the trash can. You might have to have a muse, a person whose own mind, words, or body lead you into creative states of mind.

Creativity is not a passive process. You take a step and devote yourself to a new exploration of a story and where it takes you. You open the door to creativity and commit to going where it takes you. Often, the journey is the best part of the experience. It can also be the worst. That's why artists talk about "suffering" for their art. Their creative process churns up emotions and memories that can be terribly painful but that nonetheless inspire them. Authors may take a lifetime to write a novel because of their commitment to finding truth. There are talented people who decide that the price is too steep once they begin the creative process and see the dark places it may take them. Often, it requires giving up control, facing naked emotions and then exposing them to the world. The creative mind may tap into the depths of the unconscious or spiritual source where the material is raw and unprocessed. Filtering out the meaning may be painful. It may also be joyous. Either way, the full expression of your creativity can change your life as well as the lives of those with whom you share it.

TRANSPERSONAL POWER: THE POWER OF GROUP CREATIVITY

When you tap the mental energies of those around you, there is a surge of powerful creative processing. This is why smart leaders surround themselves with innovators. You can do the same by seeking creative inspiration from friends, family, and free spirits.

A friend of mine who is an elder in a Native American tribe said dream sharing is a critical part of their problem-solving process. They tap the collective minds of tribe members whenever they face a difficult problem with no obvious solution by resolving that all tribal council members will dream about it for three nights. They meet after several days to give each person time to evaluate their dreams, and then discuss even those that don't appear to be relevant to the matter at hand. If a significant number of the members report having very similar dreams, everyone focuses on those dreams to see if a resolution might be found in their messages or symbolism. My friend offered as an example the tribe's concern about three young men who were disrespectful toward tribal values and causing concerns. Since they were not breaking laws there was no legal recourse, but the words they used hurt the spirit of the community. The council did not want to exile them, but their tolerance was at its limits. They agreed to dream about possible solutions and actions.

Six of the council members had similar dreams in which young wolf pups were taken by the eagle to its nest and confined there until they were taught the way of the spirit. All but one returned to their dens to lead a correct life. The one who remained stayed with the eagle to learn to relate to the Great Spirit. After much discussion and explanation from the shamans, it was decided that the boys would go to a retreat for three days with three elders. During that time, the leader of the gang fell ill and was rushed to the hospital where it was discovered that he had a significant brain tumor. He died, and the other two boys returned home, obviously shaken by the news and the experience. Those young men never caused problems of that nature again. That experience reinforced the tribe's belief in the power of their collective dreams to guide them to the best course of action.

The process of engaging multiple consciousnesses in creativity, especially as it pertains to group needs, works in much the same manner as the individual creative process. The four keys are still immersion, incubation, symbolic formulation, and evaluation. The group's immersion stage is one in which all the members study the quest or challenge, much as the Native American council did. A very similar way is used by our court system, in which the problem is presented from different perspectives and then evaluated by a judge or jury. I've given a lot of testimony over the years as an expert witness and I can assure you that judges, in particular, come up with some very creative solutions.

In most group incubation periods, resolutions can be found sometimes in dreams, but mostly in times of quiet contemplation. Some groups prefer listening to personal selections of music, similar to religious group processes. Some have elaborate rituals, such as the Native American Sun Dance or the conclaves held by the Roman Catholic Church's College of Cardinals. Who knows what Supreme Court justices do, but there is rarely an immediate decision on the weighty issues they must decide. Business groups convene to develop creative approaches to the problems of their organizations. Since changes in economy are always prevalent in a free-market society like ours, positive and creative solutions are a requirement for businesses to stay afloat. It is the most imaginative solution that opens up a door of opportunity that defines success. This process is repeated every day for the executive.

While evaluating the creative process calls for a multidisciplinary approach, sometimes this analysis can cause the destruction of creativity. It is often said that the design of the camel came about because God gave the responsibility of building a horse to a committee. Multiple creations do not necessarily make for the most efficient or elegant solutions. It is the wisdom of the group that decides whether or not creativity can work for their cause.

SOME FINAL THOUGHTS

If I could have one wish granted by the government (big chance of that happening), I would want every person in the nation and perhaps on this planet to have his or her life story put on a computer file. My mother-in-law, Ilene, often says as she talks about the events of her life, "I could write a book." You have a unique experience unlike any other person. You have special thoughts, passions, and dreams that only you know. Most of us constantly adjust to our surroundings, trying to fit in without losing our individuality. Still, each of our stories is unique because of the individual challenges that come in the chaos of physical demands and emotional conflicts. My favorite part of psychology is hearing the stories of my patients. Their courage and perseverance always astound me. They are my heroes.

There is no such thing as "a common life" as far as I can tell. Each life is an act of creation and a work of art. You may behave in socially accepted ways so that you never stand out from the crowd. You may never gain fame. You may never be the president of the United States. But you will express your creativity in ways that are unique to you. The role you decided to play was determined by your own view of who you are and the opportunities around you. Some may feel "ordinary." But each life has its extraordinary elements. In the end, the choices you make and the creativity you express tell the story of your life. You are the author responsible for the creation of that story.

The fact that we shape our lives by deciding how to inhabit our world excites me because it reflects the passion of the human spirit. Change is inevitable. Our bodies change and our world changes. You cannot be eighteen all your life. You cannot be exactly what you were, and you will be different in the future. Every cell in your body will change at least once every seven years. Your parents will change. You will experience losses. This is the basic law of life. No one I know has lived forever, at least in the same body. Sometimes it is the stubbornness we have to keep our brain in the same gear, refusing to let it serve us, that creates our own pain.

Creativity is not a privilege; it is a requirement if you are going to live the most passionate life possible for you. You can shut down your brain in order to avoid the pain of the challenges. If you refuse to re-create your life to take advantage of the opportunities that await you, you will suffer. Don't be stubborn. Don't let ego interfere with the full expression of your talents.

A man was caught in a huge rainstorm and a flood was certain. A neighbor came by and offered him and his family a ride to higher ground in his SUV. His family accepted the offer, but he refused by saying, "I will be saved by the Lord." Hours later, the water rose eight feet and he was sitting on the roof when a rescue boat pulled up and offered him a ride to higher ground. Again he refused with the explanation that the Lord would save him. As his house was completely submerged and he was holding on to the television antenna, a rescue helicopter hovered overhead and began lowering a rope but again he waved them off, saying God would take care of him. Instead, the water rose higher, his house collapsed, and he drowned. Then, when he met God in heaven, the man asked why he was not saved from the floodwaters. The good Lord raised an eyebrow and offered this thundering response: "I sent an SUV, a boat, and a chopper! But you were too stubborn and blind to see that they came from me!"

Your creativity is a gift from your creator. Don't be so stubborn or blind that you don't use all of the gifts sent your way. Live with passion and express your talents to their fullest. We all lose if you do not fully engage that magnificent mind of yours. We are one tribe and our power and our survival depend on the full expression of our collective creativity, intelligence, and dreams.

Twelve

SMART LOVE

C.J. was twenty-two years old, in his first job after college, and, to his puzzlement, he was suffering from depression. He could not figure out why he felt so unhappy but he knew it was affecting his performance on the job. He worried that he was making a bad impression and that it would affect his future in the business community. Yet he barely had the energy to get to work on time.

He decided to build up his physical energy in the hopes that his mental power would increase too. He went to a fitness center and began running on an indoor track. C.J. had always found that exercise lifted his spirits and eased his depression. His mood was just starting to improve as he rounded the third turn at the track, when a lightning storm knocked out the power to the building. The entire fitness center went black.

C.J. had been running easily to warm up so he stopped right away. But a woman behind him on the track had been running at a dead sprint. Natural laws of momentum came into play, and Sonja went crashing right into C.J.

In the movies, they call this "meeting cute."

The young male and the young female went sprawling on the track. Her body ended up on top of his in the dark. A very startled Sonja was the first to speak: "I am so sorry. I hope you are okay."

C.J. replied with assurance, "I'm okay. In fact, this may be the most fun I've ever had on this track, or any track for that matter!"

Sonja liked the sound of his voice and his easy humor. Since the fitness center was still dark, the two of them got up and walked to the side of the track. They talked as if they'd known each other for at least a couple of hours. When the backup generator kicked in and the lights came on, they both liked what they saw too.

C.J. had immediately been drawn to the smell, feel, and sound of this woman in the dark, and she was even more appealing in the light. Sonja had felt an immediate attraction too. They stood and talked, made it clear to each other that they were unattached romantically, and then with ease, C.J. sealed the deal. They made a date for dinner that night. Suddenly, our young male friend wasn't feeling depressed. In fact, he was downright giddy. Sonja may have knocked him off track at the gym, but she put him back on track with his life.

The courtship began that night. C.J.'s new life, one steeped in the magic of romantic love, took him to places beyond the reach of mere antidepressants. He dreamed about Sonja. He ate, drank, and slept with images of her swirling in his brain. She became his creative muse. He began to write poems and sing songs to her. Suddenly, he had a purpose to his life.

Sonja was a dedicated teacher. He admired that in her, and he knew that in order to win her heart, he would have to show that he too was serious about his career. C.J. threw himself into his job with a new vigor and purpose. He was suddenly more creative and energetic, and his stock rose dramatically with his supervisors, who promoted him. Clearly love stimulated this young man emotionally, intellectually, physically, and creatively.

LOVE AS A BRAIN STIMULANT FOR CREATIVITY

Emotional highs trigger creativity. Romantic love is the "trigger" that we most often sing about. But friendship, parenthood, and even religious faith—what is more rousing than a great gospel song?—are also common sources of creative inspiration.

Relationship dynamics, what we call "love," can be responsible for many positive mental advantages. It is only within the past ten years that we have begun to understand this mystery from a scientific standpoint.

Powerful commitment, whether to a lover, a family, a friend, or a cause, is often the catalyst for achieving higher mental performance. This phenomenon played itself out on the big screen through Russell Crowe's excellent portrayal of Jim Braddock in the movie *Cinderella Man*, the story of how a mediocre boxer found his inspiration to become the world champion. The changing energy that marked the success of the real man's climb to fame was the awareness of the path for his family's sake. That powerful emotional commitment fueled his drive for success. The phrase "You are the champion of my heart," supposedly said to this great athlete by his wife, is indicative of the power of faith and hope. Being placed in the role of hero in the name of love has always been a major source of physical and mental power.

Happiness is another emotion that triggers creativity. When you are loved by another, it is a powerful affirmation of your worthiness. That's what Norah Jones is expressing when she sings, "And then I wonder who I am without the warm touch of your hand." Dean Martin and a host of others put it more bluntly when they sang, "You're nobody 'til somebody loves you. You're nobody 'til somebody cares."

There is nothing more fulfilling and uplifting than having someone you love return your feelings. It also does wonders for the brain. Emotions stimulate neurological connections, even within the "memories" of each nerve cell. The idea that nerve cells possess memory is a new concept developed by Dr. Itzhak Fried of the University of California, Los Angeles. (These results were published in *Nature*, June 23, 2005.)

Neurons work with information, particularly cells in the medial temporal lobe, an area critical to forming long-term memories. In their innovative research methodology, Fried's group studied three men and five women as they viewed famous and nonfamous people, landmarks, animals, and foods. After noting pronounced electrical responses in at least one neuron, the scientists performed additional trials to study different neuron reactions from different angles and situations. For example, in one person a single neuron fired strongly only in response to various images of Jennifer Aniston alone; however, when Brad Pitt was in the picture, that neuron refused to fire.

The bottom line is that memory can be stored within the neurons, and with stimulation, will activate more memory and associations. In this pathway of understanding, at the most basic levels, love and emotions can help both memory and cognitive functions. It is also the driving force of happiness that promotes the optimism and the sense of limitless potential.

This bit of neural information is just one piece of what causes the overall increased flow of endorphins that are produced with high excitement, especially sexual stimulation. Endorphins are internal painkillers. They work like the body's homemade morphine. If there is no pain that requires numbing, the endorphins, bless 'em, head straight for the pleasure centers of the brain. They account for the "runner's high" experienced by joggers.

WHAT IS LOVE?

There are over one thousand definitions of love. *The Reader's Digest Great Encyclopedia Dictionary* describes it as a deep devotion or affection for another person or persons. The Greeks noted three kinds of love. *Agape* is unconditional and freely given; *philo* is a friend's love; and *eros* is based more on sexual or creative expression. We love different people in different ways. If you had two children, Timmy and Tonia, you would have a Timmy-love and a Tonia-love. If you loved your God, you would have a God-love.

The act of loving someone can be directly observed through the brain and throughout your body. Your immune system sparkles with excitement that creates a better defense against disease, and you actually gain muscular strength. Your creativity soars from the stimulation of the right brain so that even males begin to integrate their intellectual vision with creativity.

The intriguing aspect is the effect on the beloved, which is not as scientifically verified. We know that newborn babies thrive when loved, while those without love tend to suffer in mental strengths. We know that increased neurological activities in individual brain maps are significant when love is directed toward them through prayer and directed imagery. If the energy of love could manifest cognitive changes, then we would certainly have a major resource for all of our children, and Alzheimer's disease would probably be stamped out. I am not saying this doesn't happen. I just don't know how it happens—yet. But the point I want to emphasize is that evidence indicates that those who love the most gain the greatest benefit cognitively.

IS YOUR BRAIN IN LOVE?

This questionnaire will help you assess whether you have a level of love strong enough to enhance your creative powers. Please indicate whether or not you would agree (A), agree but not totally (MA), agree slightly (SA), or not agree at all (DA) with these statements.

1. I have a very strong love for someone to whom I devote my full energies, regardless of what I am doing.

   A   MA   SA   DA

2. I am inspired by my love relationship and devote time to create music, poetry, or some form of art to my expression of it.

   A   MA   SA   DA

3. The love relationship makes me happy and optimistic, regardless of the situation.

   A   MA   SA   DA

4. I feel that I want to be the best person I can at everything to be worthy of such a love.

   A   MA   SA   DA

5. I am the champion of a love relationship, so I am strong in commitment and courage in whatever I am doing.

   A   MA   SA   DA

6. I often discover that during the day, my mind wanders into my love relationship, and I find myself integrating those thoughts with my other work.

   A   MA   SA   DA

7. Music is more important to me with the experience of my love relationship.

   A   MA   SA   DA

8. I often remember small details about my love relationship, which deepens my need for it.

   A   MA   SA   DA

9. I would fiercely defend my love relationship against all odds, even to death itself.

   A   MA   SA   DA

10. I have a reason to work harder and learn more because of my love relationship.

    A   MA   SA   DA

11. I find myself more intrigued with life's questions because of my love relationship.

    A   MA   SA   DA

12. My greatest joy comes when I can express myself within my love relationship.

    A   MA   SA   DA

Scoring:

For each "A" you circled, give a credit of 3 points, for each "MA," give a credit of 2 points, and for each "SA" you circled, give a credit of 1 point. Add the items for a total in the range of 0 to 36, and compare your score to the ranges below.

Score	Meaning
30–36	Your love is definitely a stimulating factor in your brain for greater creativity and cognition.
22–29	Your love relationship holds some power for developing more creativity and optimistic feelings in yourself.
14–21	Your love relationship may be an asset to your creativity, but may also be causing you some stress.
8–13	Your love relationship is exerting very minimal impact on your creativity and mental activities.
0–7	You either do not have a love relationship or it is not a factor in enhancing your creative or cognitive abilities.

A BRIEF HISTORY OF THE PSYCHOLOGY OF LOVE ENERGIES

Love leads to other things, of course. Freud, the original "love doctor," came up with the concept of *libido*. He believed that the major source of psychological energy was the sex drive. Freud viewed this natural and instinctive energy source as the ultimate survival mechanism of the species. It certainly is more fun than "fight or flight" in the minds of most people.

Of course, some consider the sex drive to be a "beastly" or primitive aspect of the naked ape's makeup. In many circles it is still considered uncouth to speak of one's passions and sexual needs in public. In Victorian times, a woman who was open about her sexuality risked being diagnosed as "hysterical" and thrown in a mental institution.

The fact that Freud never "cured" anyone of their sex drive doesn't seem to have diminished the popularity of his theories. One of his followers did try to establish the scientific validity of Freud's work and he turned up some interesting material. Wilhelm Reich attached electrodes to all parts of the body in order to measure how much energy was generated by the sexual parts. He tracked the flow of energy when his human guinea pigs had orgasms. He confirmed that the "orgone energy" flowed in linear paths in the body, and that when there appeared to be blockage of these energies, disease often occurred. This concept is very similar to Chinese medicine's concepts of energy flow blockages created by disease. The most fascinating finding is the linkage made between the blockages and related psychological characteristics. It was claimed that a person who has blockages in the energy flow in the stomach also would have corresponding "issues" of insecurity and fear of abandonment. Patients with colon and digestive tract problems were believed to have corresponding psychological problems of obsession. A general topology of the body related to blockages in the energy field is presented below:

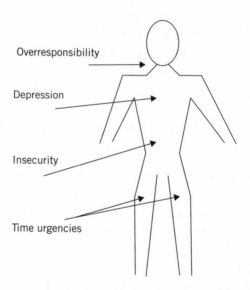

Overresponsibility

Depression

Insecurity

Time urgencies

Dr. Reich then became interested in how these blockages affected cancer, because it made sense to him that tumors were mainly blocked healing forces. He invented the ambitious "Orgone boxes," large enough for patients to sit inside. The boxes were reported to heal twenty-six terminal cases by means of Reich's theoretical energy process. Unfortunately, Reich's science wasn't well received by the establishment. He was arrested for transporting his healing boxes across state lines and convicted of contempt of court because he refused to attend the trial. He died in a prison cell, a box of a different sort.

Dr. Reich was not the only person fascinated by the "electro-energy" body of mental health. Franz Anton Mesmer, the source of the term "mesmerize," felt that the body and mind were basically conduits for magnetic forces of energy. In his mesmerizing demonstrations, he would have men and women sit down, face each other, and interlock their knees. They then were encouraged to feel the powerful electric currents generated. Many of the people would faint from the powerful experiences. Imagine what the same people might have done if he'd asked them to do some "dirty dancing" like today's teens.

In spite of the theatrics of these early dabblers and scientists, there are still many who believe in the validity of energy flow through the body and brain. It is not something condoned by traditional medicine or the American Medical Association, but nontraditional healers and even some free-thinking medical doctors continue to test the concept of energetic flows for mental health. The Chinese practice of acupuncture is based on the belief in energy flows. The acupuncture needles are used to correct blockages of the flow. Pain, anxiety, depression, and stress have been documented as disorders that can be helped by these methods. Touch therapy, SHEN therapy, and Reiki therapies have shown effective shifts in these same psychological states, releasing undue challenges to the natural flow of mental energy (tai chi).

What I call *love energy* is beneficial to various forms of mental activities. There is scientific evidence that the emotional stimuli of love and affection can and will produce powerful effects. If you know your history, especially that of ancient Rome and Greece, you know that nations have gone to war over such truths. The stories of Cleopatra and Mark Antony on the war over Helen of Troy come to mind.

HOW TO GET YOUR BRAIN TO FALL IN LOVE

I am sure no one disputes that the emotion of romantic love has an impact on the brain and its functions. They don't call it "lovesick" for no reason. I believe a certain wise owl noted that love that blooms in the spring can result in one becoming "twitterpated"—at least that's the term used in the classic Disney animated movie *Bambi*. So we know lovesickness is basic to all animal nature, even the cartoon versions.

The real question is how to activate the mighty forces of love. It's an age-old question, but the answers are complex. I have read some of the leading religious perspectives on the topic. I've come to appreciate the spiritual benefits of love. I am particularly fond of the Christian belief that "God is love."

But how do you create a "loving" brain, or a mental state that is equally exhilarating? You don't need a romantic lover to feel the warmth of love and connection, but it helps! Direct experience is the best, but here are some other avenues for plugging into the "love connection":

1. *Love is a choice.* You can love anyone you want. I love my patients for their genuine stories. I do not voice these thoughts nor do I act on them. I do not want them to return my love, either. I love them because my contact and work with them is so rewarding for me.

2. *You don't have to act or react to love.* You can love someone for the way in which they reflect God's love or you can love their spirituality, their soul, without having to act on these feelings. The principle here is that when you tap into your brain's capacity for love, it can be solely for your internal pleasure.

3. *You can experience the "loving" brain through imagery.* I have experienced the challenges of being caregiver to my mother during her decline into fronto-temporal dementia. I've discovered that love never goes away. Even when my mother could no longer express her love, it is always there in my memories. That love allows me to continue to see her as the woman who cared for me as a child. Love has a great shelf life in that regard. As the song goes, "We'll always have the memories." The mind is kind in its constant replaying of her image for me. I can repeat the movies of my experiences forever. They are as real as life. They are my life, as is she.

4. *Music and dance stimulate the loving brain.* Music provides acoustical stimulation to the brain that triggers emotions. Imagery and music go hand in hand for the stimulation of love-related feelings. Old songs in which love memories are brought forward into the present can enhance brain function, especially memory. Dancing is a physical reminder of those feelings, especially the rhythmic beats that arouse our most basic instincts.

5. *Commit to the selfless attitude of love.* There is no doubt that the maintenance of a loving brain takes commitment. What creates the

most conflicts in marriages is the loss of the devotion to each other's happiness. It is too easy to make other things a priority when there are bills to pay, children to care for, and all of the other distractions of daily life. Then there are the obnoxious behaviors that we all bring to the table, or the couch, or the bedroom. Sometimes restoring that "loving feeling" requires recommitting to each other's happiness as a mutual priority. As a marriage counselor, I saw that the loss of that commitment can lead to the breakdown not only of a relationship but of the mental strength of both parties. You actually get less capable of making good decisions, especially for the relationship, when your love fades. You get anxious and depressed largely because you lack the "love" resources that pump up your brain.

6. *Happiness is a choice.* You cannot change what happens to you, but you can always change how you react to what happens. As a boy, I would go to my father with stories of other kids picking on me. He'd listen to me talk about the unfairness and injustice with great empathy for about ten minutes. But at the end of it, he would say, "Okay, now get happy." He was telling me that I had that choice. I could change my attitude into a more productive state. And I learned to do just that.

It is true that we are the captains of our emotions. Even prisoners have the freedom to be happy. Even those in poverty can choose an attitude of love. In research surveys on happiness, class and circumstance make no difference. Rich people are no happier than poor people. The bottom line is that when we choose happiness and loving attitudes we improve our health and our abilities to make better choices.

7. *It takes courage to love.* While I could extol the benefits of adopting a loving brain for months, I also know that some people still won't believe me. If you were truly spiritual and accepted that there was a God who loved you, that knowledge would allow you to rejoice every day. But some people cannot accept that anyone could love them for who they are. When I was director of research at the University of Arkansas Rehabilitation Research and Training Center, we investigated how individuals accept or reject unconditional positive

regard. We found that not one of the thousands of people we studied would accept unconditional love from another person. It was too risky and scary. It seems that unless they had experience from some other loving environment, they could not conceive of such a thing. I can understand this because we begin our life in a world of big people (parents) who control our existence. They punish us for behaviors we shouldn't do by telling us we are "bad." The message is clear from the time we are five years old: "You are essentially bad if you don't repress all of your natural urges and feelings." It takes courage to love others unconditionally because you have to love yourself unconditionally. It is easier to keep your brain in neutral because of the possibilities of fooling yourself into thinking you are good, and dealing with the guilt of having that feeling.

8. *Be aware of love and positive experiences.* I like to see whether my patients are pessimists or optimists by applying the half-empty or half-full cup test. I challenge each of them to make a list of the hundred good things that will happen to them every day. The idea is that we perceive what we select to perceive. If you choose to, you can decide to overlook the songs of the birds, the images of the clouds, and the unique courage within each person. I tend to stand in awe of most people, simply because of the challenges they face every day. Everyone has someone die. Everyone has to make critical decisions. Everyone has to sacrifice and overcome problems. Yet we also have the power to focus on the beauty of each day, and the love others give us that bolsters our brains and brings joy to our lives.

9. *Inspiration reignites that loving feeling.* I don't believe that the world's religious centers exist just as symbols of faith. From our earliest times, humans have sought spiritual inspiration with rituals, celebration, and meditation. Nature is another "temple" for spiritual inspiration. The Grand Canyon, Yosemite, the Rockies, Malibu, the Black Hills, and other wonders of the world have inspired people for generations.

Every day, in many ways, men and women find inspiration that triggers the brain's capacity to love. People are born again into a new life of creativity, spirituality, and love of others. Inspired, they create new goals and new pathways for fulfillment. I've been especially touched by people who have rebounded after hard falls. Some I've known have reached heights of success only to be overcome by the temptations and excesses of fame and celebrity.

Probably the most memorable for me was a fellow I'd known since high school. At nineteen, he had struggled with a deep sense of unworthiness, and was frightfully shy and timid. He struggled every day to meet people, but his insecurity was a major hurdle. I knew him only as an acquaintance in west Texas. He became a bass player for Buddy Holly and for a time, he soared with his talents. Then he took a fall because of drug abuse.

There may be some irony in the fact that the very talent that led to his decline into drug addiction eventually pulled him out. He returned to the joy of his musical talents. He tapped into this deep love and his brain responded. This man began to learn that his music was the way he could show love toward others and reach a level of intimacy in his heart. It helped that he had understanding and loyal friends, such as Johnny Cash and Willie Nelson, who were ready to stand on stage with him when he was back on his feet. Waylon Jennings died recently, but he exited this world to the sound of music in the air and with much love in his heart—all of it reflected in the hearts of countless others.

Thirteen

RAISING A FAMILY OR A NATION TO FULL POTENTIAL

Working on *Dr. Phil* has many wonderful perks. It is especially gratify-ing to know that we help a lot of people on and off the show. People from around the nation e-mail our Web site hoping to get on the show, not for the public exposure (if you see Dr. Phil hammering them you wonder why anyone would ever want to come face-to-face with him), but because they are desperate and stuck. More than 17,000 inquiries come in every week, making it difficult to get through them, but these e-mails and letters do not go unheeded. We deal with as many as we can. Their stories touch us all.

Delores (a fictitious name for privacy concerns) had a particularly compelling tale. She came to us for help in desperation. Her family's survival was in jeopardy. Delores was the victim of sexual abuse by an uncle. She was only thirteen when he talked her into having sex with his friends. He took payment for the abuse she endured. Not surprisingly, Delores was pregnant at the age of fifteen. Her sleazy uncle nearly killed her by poisoning her because she exposed his abuse. She was on the verge of death for six weeks and lost her baby, a terrible experience for anyone. She had a deep need for revenge.

She felt like a "dirty tramp" because of the abuse she had endured. Sadly, she became pregnant again at the age of eighteen. The marriage that followed lasted eight years, but it was unloving. Her husband, Carl, a full-blown alcoholic at fifteen, never finished the tenth grade. He was physically abusive and relied on Delores's skills as a home care provider to support him and their three children. You might say that Carl was a replacement for her uncle—except that he was never interested in sex, except when drunk.

Delores had survived some very tough times. She came to us, not about her own problems but because her eight-year-old son, Joseph, desperately needed help. He had been diagnosed with attention deficit disorder at the age of five. His school had kicked him out and would not let him back in until he could find a doctor to manage his problems. Delores's middle child, Alicia, was a beautiful five-year-old. The kindergarten student suffered from insecurity. She wet the bed and stayed close to home much of the time. This was clearly a very nervous kid whose future was grim. The two-year-old, Eric, was not yet affected by his chaotic environment, yet his mother, who had been conditioned to expect the worst, checked him for symptoms every day.

Delores told us that she traced all of her problems back to her uncle and her suffering at his hands. When she came to us, she could not stop talking about the abuse she had suffered. She was consumed by her sordid experiences in the past. Carl was sullen at first. He expected to be confronted on his own abuse and alcoholism. As a child, his father and uncle would take turns beating him in their drunken rages. He ran away from home at the age of twelve. He felt that if he had graduated from high school he would have had a chance to escape his past. He managed to support himself for three years until he became discouraged and quit.

This family was deeply troubled. Clearly the parents were repeating their histories of abuse. If this scenario continued it was certain that the children would be worse off than their parents. This cycle could have gone on for generations. This was a challenge, even with all the resources we have. Instead of making Joseph the target patient, we made a "project" of the whole family. To their credit, it took tremendous courage for this family to face their challenges and agree to make the changes necessary to reverse their downward spiral. It was not an easy process, and there were many complications, but we were able to work together and achieve remarkable results because this family took responsibility for their own healing.

Delores took a major step by correcting her diet, which helped her clear her head and her thinking. She established a new identity as a nurturer. She stopped blaming her past for her present. She discovered the joy of controlling her own destiny.

Carl was the biggest surprise to us all as he confessed his fear of failure and agreed that his alcoholism was a form of self-medication. He quickly realized that he could be a hero instead of a loser. He got into a vocational rehabilitation program, trained as a computer analyst, and, in another twist, ended up getting certified as a nurse. It turned out to be a good combination of skills. He moved swiftly into hospital administration.

Joseph, it turned out, did not have ADD. He did have high levels of anxiety and impulse control problems. He also rated high in intelligence tests, despite his poor performance in school. He was wary but quickly warmed to our staff. He also proved to have a keen sense of humor. Joseph was obviously a smart kid and not yet trapped by the same despair that had nearly overwhelmed his parents.

Joseph quickly learned relaxation and breathing techniques. We also taught him methods for focusing his mind through martial arts training. And finally, we showed him how to calm his mind and his mood with soothing music and resonance devices. It was gratifying when he began to enjoy schoolwork and even excel in it.

Alicia was also anxiety ridden, but her needs were less obvious because she had yet to develop the language skills needed for in-depth interviews and analysis. Nevertheless, with the help of a counselor, she, too, responded to therapy. Finally, this child learned to trust adults. It was a major breakthrough when she accepted support and abandoned her fears.

This was a cooperative effort. We invested our time, training, and expertise and this family showed tremendous courage and commitment. None of the positive changes would have occurred if Delores had not made the choice to dramatically alter the course of her life and that of her family. In doing that, both parents accepted responsibility, a huge shift in attitude. And as a result, they set up their children and generations to come on a path to a much, much more hopeful future. The entire family rallied around this effort, forming a bond of love and pride in their role in reversing their fortunes.

THE INDOMITABLE FAMILY POTENTIAL

In an "Indomitable Family" each member is a star. Each member has a life filled with hope and passion. Each parent and child feels the support, love, and nurturing of the other family members. Most of all, the members have the freedom and resources to maximize their talents and opportunities. It is the parents' responsibility to create this environment for their children as well as for themselves.

It takes more than good intentions and a mission statement to raise a family today. Parents often have to recognize where their first challenge lies. Their own dysfunctional family experiences may have rendered them unfit for parental duty unless they address their issues first. When Dr. Phil asked me to consult on his book *Family First*, one of the first things we did was review the questions parents had submitted to his Web site. After going through more than twenty thousand inquiries from parents, I was dumbfounded. More than half indicated that they had not a clue how to deal with their children's problems and needs. These parents appeared to be standing on the edge of a cliff, fully prepared to jump if a problem arose.

The family ideal had obviously changed, along with family values. The bonds of family members were strained to the point of breaking, or already snapped. "Home is where the heart is" had become "Home is where the heart attack begins." Working parents, overscheduled kids, meals on the run, weekends with everyone flying in different directions, television, video games, status cars, and house payments that rival the budgets of small nations have all contributed to a new model: The Stressed Family.

Today's typical dysfunctional family is led by parents who not only don't have a plan, they don't have a clue. With most who come to me for assistance, it is not a matter of starting from ground zero. We start deep in a hole and try to crawl up to ground zero. A shocking number of parents come from dysfunctional families so that they have no models for proper parenting. Paternal and maternal instincts are virtually extinct.

Today's families are all too often focused on their limitations rather than on their strengths. The blame game is the latest parent trap. They are on the defensive constantly for their children's failings academically, socially, and physically. And then, of course, parents tend to blame themselves. Often when a child is diagnosed with attention deficit disorder, parents immediately look inward and recall how they had their own challenges with short attention spans. So they blame themselves for their child's ADD.

Blame has no healing powers, whether self-inflicted or injected by all-too-willing outsiders. Focusing on problems is another prescription for failure. I tell parents that if they really want to heal their family and set it on a more hopeful course, they first must make the decision to stop looking in the rearview mirror. You can't go forward while looking back. A crash is inevitable. In fact, if your family wants to be miserable, I can offer you these specific steps to guarantee it. If you want to stay stuck, these are the ways:

1. Compare your family to a "perfect family" down the street or on the tube. There are no perfect families. There are indomitable families, which you can be, but they are not perfect by any means.

2. Pick out a person who you think has a perfect family and envy him or her. Assume they have no problems and just sulk over your misfortune. Everyone has challenges.

3. Choose some superhero, like an athlete, a movie star, or a rich person, and compare your lives. Be sure to berate yourself for not achieving as much.

4. If you have any physical or emotional problems, such as concentration problems or anxieties, be sure and blame all your failures on these limits.

5. Restrict yourself from joy and happiness at all costs.

Okay, so I am being facetious here. I don't believe that you want to go to the Dark Side. Otherwise, you would not have picked up this book, nor would you have read this far.

I have never met a parent who did not want the best for their children and family. Most parents sacrifice a great deal for their children. Many give them far too much in the way of material things. The pressures are incredible, I know. Kids have such high expectations today because of advertising and marketing directed at them. Even Christmas has gotten out of hand. There are usually way too many gifts provided. Kids have come to expect it, rather than appreciating it. Parents should not feel obligated to live up to impossible expectations that are set by corporations in search of profits. Families need to set their own expectations based on values and principles, not material possessions or status.

THE INDOMITABLE FAMILY ASSESSMENT

If you want to put a plan in place to create an indomitable family experience, you will need to begin with an assessment of where you are right now. Here is a tool for doing that. Please rate the following statements to indicate if they are Always True (AT), Sometimes True (ST), Rarely True (RT), or Never True (NT) of your behavior and attitudes.

1. I have always thought that if I let my children have the freedom to do whatever they need to do, they would develop a positive self-image.

    AT   ST   RT   NT

2. I was abused or traumatized at an early age, and have a problem that infringes on my being an indomitable parent.

    AT   ST   RT   NT

3. I have to make a living and have obligations that make my family the second priority now; maybe things will be different later.

    AT   ST   RT   NT

4. I find that I spend most of my time correcting and telling my children "no," because they misbehave.

    AT   ST   RT   NT

5. I do not have goals for my family because I am just trying to live one day to the next without pain.

    AT   ST   RT   NT

6. I do not know all the strengths of my family, but I do know their limitations.

    AT   ST   RT   NT

7. Life is so stressed I cannot think of creating positive steps for a closer family for the time being.

    AT   ST   RT   NT

8. I think my children and mate are usually thinking how bad a parent I am, and even resent me.

    AT   ST   RT   NT

9. As a family we do not have stories that we often share and enjoy and that serve as family esteem.

    AT   ST   RT   NT

10. I don't get the respect I want from my family, and I want people to know that I am right.

    AT   ST   RT   NT

11. I use hollering as my main method of discipline and to reinforce behavior.

    AT   ST   RT   NT

12. I don't care what my children do as long as they respect others and don't cause problems.

    AT   ST   RT   NT

13. I am resentful when I sacrifice for the family and they do not acknowledge it.

    AT   ST   RT   NT

14. I act like a hero for my family.

AT   ST   RT   NT

15. I do not have a plan if or when a crisis happens.

AT   ST   RT   NT

Scoring:

For each Always True response (AT), assign a credit of 3, for each Some-times True response, assign a credit of 2, and for each Rarely True re-sponse (RT), assign a credit of 1. Total your credits for a sum in the range between 0 and 45, and compare your score to the following ranges.

Range	Interpretation
38–45	This score indicates that your family is in a downward spiral. It is critical that you stop, reverse course, and begin to tap their potential.
28–37	This score indicates that your family is lacking a plan for tapping into its strengths and moving forward. It is time to find solutions and move in a new direction.
20–27	This score indicates that your family lacks a plan to move to higher levels of achievement by removing limitations that are self-imposed.
10–19	This score indicates that your family is confused as to how to develop a positive family plan for the benefit of all members. The next step is to begin to recognize each other's abilities and potentials.
0–9	This score implies that your family has an indomitable bond.

Evaluate your answers and where your family is headed according to the scoring. The bottom line is that if you want to create an indomitable family and turn your lives around, you need to have a plan. You can't get new and better results by doing the same things over and over. So it is time to change direction. You may have difficulty getting everyone in the family to buy into the new plan. If you have to drag them kicking and screaming into a better life, that is your job. Nobody said being a grownup would be easy. So grow up, get up, and get going!

THREE STEPS TOWARD CREATING AN INDOMITABLE FAMILY

The good news is that I've already taken you through the steps to creating an indomitable family. We've looked at clearing the brain, releasing psychological barriers, and enhancing creativity, which are all critical to this process of regeneration and reversal of the family fortunes.

Step One: The Neurological Evolution of the Brain

The reality of diminished opportunities and the making of poor choices are intimately related to brain blockage. Whether caused by physical or psychological trauma, shutting down is the brain's response to some form of extreme pain. The brain does not jump back to life easily. Many times it needs to be jump-started.

When the brain shuts down, the interconnections begin to withdraw. Certain brain cells go into hibernation. The longer your brain hibernates, the more stimulation it will take to wake it up. To get your family's brains firing on all cylinders, it may be necessary to get a healthier meal plan. I recommend a diet high in protein. Exercise to stimulate the system is also a good thing. Music that gets the whole family going is another great inspirational and motivational force. A family focus on spirituality can also be a positive step.

Family games—not video games—can be a great way of bringing everyone together. Laughter and friendly competition are healing tools. I recommend open-book Scrabble because it helps improve limited vocabularies while requiring strategy.

Family rituals enhance esteem and create a social rhythm, especially if you establish consistent meeting times and provide support for those who need special assistance and considerations. Everyone's brains will function better in a comforting and loving setting.

I encourage you to measure everyone's progress. Establish a goal so that you can celebrate achievements. When someone learns a new song or masters the multiplication tables, make it a family event to encourage further growth. When a course is passed or a problem solved, it is time for festivity.

Step Two: Releasing Psychological Barriers

After your brains are in full gear and you can make constructive choices again, do yourselves a favor and clear out all of the baggage of guilt and shame. Now is not the time to look back. Focus on the future. It is time to feel joy and freedom and optimism. The need for doing this cannot be overstated. Individuals with histories of drug abuse report that their brain has to be "dry" for a period before they can look to the future and take constructive action. Children who have been given medication for attention deficit disorder or depression also need to be "clean" of their drugs for a period before their brains return to a more natural balance. These drugs numb their senses and their emotions. If Johnny has been on an antidepressant since the age of twelve, his emotional state will return to that of a twelve-year-old for a period after he withdraws from the drugs. Of course, the issues of medications with children are complex. Drugs can be a great tool, but usually not a complete answer. My motto of "pills without skills lead to later crisis" has been supported by my clinical experience as well as other studies. Medications can and do serve vital functions, especially in critical times when a child needs immediate help. But the job is not done until the child's skills are developed to compensate for limitations.

It might be helpful to create new, affectionate nicknames for each other to signify the new beginning. It is common among many civilizations to have a renaming ritual when a person reaches adulthood. Some Native American tribes have as many as seven developmental rituals for name changing. In the United States, women often change their names at the time of marriage. I remember a significant change in myself when I was called "Doctor" for the first time. The military uses titles to signify rank. It could be a good family tradition to bestow new nicknames as a way of honoring family members for having the courage and strength to change their lives for the better.

There is also value in releasing the burden of our limitations in family rituals. We can surrender the labels attached to us and, in the process, release the guilt or shame that accompanies them. This is especially important for someone who has broken a taboo, such as incest or murder. Someone who has violated the family trust will need forgiveness before it will be possible to move on.

Step Three: Enhanced Creativity in Social Relationships and Life Planning

With the brain functioning in high gear and the psychological barriers removed, it is time for creative new beginnings that nurture stronger relationships, greater trust, deeper love, and true forgiveness. Parents should be recognized and honored as the wise elders that they are at this stage. This is the definition of the hero's journey, the source of light and the seed for generations to come. You can change course for the benefit of your children and their children and beyond. You will be able to do what previous generations have failed at because of poor parenting.

THE REBIRTH OF A TORN NATION

The trials of a family and their redemption are one thing. What if a whole nation has been abused and corrupted? Is war the solution to political fears and struggles? As an optimist, I believe that nations can be healed without further bloodshed. Consider the following scenario.

Imagine, if you will, two children, Thomas and Fran, sitting hand-in-hand in a small room with dozens of other children as two busy women are trying to find places where these kids can sleep tonight. Thomas, twelve, is staring into space and feeling the pain from the large lump on his head where he was knocked unconscious when he tried to defend his younger sister from being raped by one of the soldiers who attacked their home and killed their parents in full view of the children. Fran, ten, is sleeping now with her head on her brother's shoulder. She had cried most of the three hours they had been waiting in the room holding her bloodstained dress, but her fatigue finally claimed her fear. We know that when they do finally go back to school, their minds will still be fighting the images that will block their attention. Toxins of depression and fear have rendered their minds numb, making them feel like failures and deflating their senses of self even more.

The fact is that in ten more years these same children will likely be doing the same horrible things to their enemies. The cycle will continue. Trauma creates chaos in the brain, shutting it down. When this occurs, we stop maturing. We develop destructive attitudes. We lose competence. We become easy targets for manipulative leaders. If you walk through a prison you will see individuals whose brains barely respond to offerings of love and support. Their brains have been so weakened by a lack of nurturing that they have little chance for survival.

I know about Thomas and Fran because I have seen the impact of war on families and individuals. I know rehabilitation works when proper methods are used. It takes three steps:

1. Recharging the brain's power

2. Eliminating the emotional obstacles to empowerment

3. Igniting creativity and opening the door for new opportunities.

I call these three steps "The Renaissance Horizon 2012 Project." My program has served as a major source of inspiration and hope. It has been recommended for countries in chaos, such as Iraq, Afghanistan, and parts of Africa. This is a real mission for a world shift to free the potential of the human spirit instead of repeating an endless cycle of hatred and violence, the ingredients of failure.

THE NEUROLOGICAL EVOLUTION OF THE BRAIN

There is a good reason why the United States has for many years avoided war on its own land. We saw the devastation of the Civil War and the damage inflicted on our citizens. We have seen the horrible effects of a lack of creativity in our approach to rebuilding nations and their governments. The aftereffects of war are certainly the most challenging for both a nation and the individuals.

The Renaissance Horizon 2012 Project develops culturally relevant programs designed specifically for the neurological development of citizens. The greatest needs are both physical and mental health services, but this does not mean merely calming people with drugs. Instead, this program seeks to awaken them to joy and pleasure again. We focus on providing healthy diets, the most appropriate kind of exercise and music, and the development of group and family cohesion.

Anyone dazed from shock and stress may find self-help programs confusing. We offer group and individual programs that first address neurological needs and healing of the mind. These programs might resemble spa-like activities, such as group meditation, imagery, movement, etc. Group classes in dietary needs and sleeping aids are available. Even musical experiences are provided that soothe the anxieties and inspire hope.

The Renaissance Horizon 2012 Project also offers professionally trained native citizens who provide mental health services. We provide desensitization services in which traumatic memories can be detached from fears and crippling emotional associations. These use devices for relaxation as well as professional treatment models. We employ powerful cognitive approaches to confront irrational reactions that can immobilize opportunities in a new nation.

The focus is a training model designed to develop the minds of new leaders and directors. This line of modeling is not new to human nature. The Egyptians had similar intentions with their "king-making" practices in ancient times, although it was limited to a small group of potential heirs. Wealthy families have often trained their heirs in the use of power and compassion. The armed forces have their officer training programs for similar reasons. This concept has its roots in the philosophy that to be a good leader and citizen it is best to have rational and empathic sensitivities to the needs of the people served.

Direct counseling is actually a lower priority in this program because most counseling models are based on "working through issues of conflict." While this work is admirable and helpful, my research review revealed that the more immediate needs are for nurturing the cognitive abilities of these individuals for best judgment and focus. One of the lowest priorities would be reframing an old memory or looking backward to understand one's history. The design that works is to maintain a forward focus for the opportunities and development of positive plans.

USING CREATIVITY IN CONFLICT RESOLUTION

The accomplishment of increased cognitive and emotional maturation is satisfying. The real benefit is the creation of a new nation that seeks innovative ideas for the benefit of all. Like individuals, every nation has unique needs. Each culture is different. Combining different cultures generates a tremendous array of talents and abilities. These various viewpoints can be the fuel for conflict, but rational interchange is how we evolve. Certainly the conflicts between Thomas Jefferson and Alexander Hamilton in this country's formation spurred very hot issues, but their resolution created the nation.

As we discussed in a previous chapter, *immersion* is the process in which issues are studied and debated. Every person considers every link to the formulation of programs and implications. Emotional passion is endured and often reinforced in order to emphasize the issues that need prioritization. Ideas are sought from the public occasionally in the form of expert testimony, and consultants are available for their information.

The *incubation* period can be extended for whatever appears to be a practical period. Sometimes prayer and meditation accompany this process, lending a spiritual perspective. Political pressure certainly can influence decisions. Deliberations are common. Occasionally letters and other communications are sent in from the public sector so that people can register their thoughts and feelings.

The third step considers the results of the *formulations,* questions, and challenges. Concrete conclusions are gathered as potential creative directions and solutions for the community. Positions are written and a plan is put in place with the resources of the collective minds. Votes are cast and a vehicle is designed to fulfill the creative output. Agencies may be formed, committees may be selected, teams may be assigned, and individuals may be directed to carry out one or more creative proposals.

The *evaluation* phase comes in many forms, but with a creative government, all endeavors are subject to proof of success. We can and have repealed laws that don't work. We can amend programs that could work better. We can reconstruct programs that are no longer needed or create a bigger vision for them. This constant evaluation enables governments to change to meet new needs. The nation that is insensitive to change or lacks creativity will enable its own destruction. This is one lesson of history.

SOME FINAL THOUGHTS

This chapter offers broad perspectives and a very optimistic scenario. I do not pretend to know the secrets of politics, but I do know that irrational approaches do not serve families or nations well. Hitler and Stalin may have inspired their countries to new levels of prosperity and power, but the destruction that resulted from their policies offers ample testimony that governments based on fear and greed will implode into their own corrupt core.

As children of the universe, the majority of people on this earth believe we have a purpose for living in this realm of consciousness. That purpose could be mere survival as a species, but my belief lies in a more hopeful evolution. I believe we exist to create a better world for those who come after us. We must be willing to sacrifice for a more peaceful and loving existence. Many soldiers have given their lives so that we might live in a better world. It is an honorable thing they have done. The paths to this imagined world have been presented by greater minds than my own. Perhaps if someone had, this book would never have been written or needed.

I am an optimistic person and truly believe that we are on the crest of a new world. The sciences of the brain, the heart, and the soul will continue to merge to form a healing process from which we will surface as better human beings. Through the processes noted in this book, each of us can gain rather than lose our vitalities. As our collective self-discoveries and creativities mesh with each other, the world has the real possibility of using wars and turmoil to find a higher and more healing plane of experience. We have seen how the outpouring of resources to hurricane victims strengthens all of us. We have seen how the courage of caretakers can inspire us to become more compassionate. Each of us can become one of the heroes of the new era. This is a time in which we can learn to become greater than we thought we could be, and reach the next level in which we are closer to what God intended us to become.

EPILOGUE

The content and exercises to strengthen cognitive abilities could continue for another three or four volumes, but I have stopped here because these are the most robust activities that I can point to after years of research. There are and will be pills designed to elevate cognitive functions to some degree and no doubt they will have effect. I am not an antidrug guy by any means, and I look forward to that day when everyone's brains, including mine, will function at 100 percent for a lifetime. My caution is that when you start taking an external substance for anything, you can be pretty sure of what you hope it will do, but there are bound to be surprises, some possibly undesirable.

The secret formula is balance. For example, there are pills available today that extend your memory, but there are some things I do not want to remember. I do not want to remember the pain I had when I broke my nose four times in football. I do not want to remember the depression I witnessed on my father's face when he failed in business. Your brain has the capacity to make that decision for you as to what you need to remember and what to forget. This ability is the natural way mothers forget the pain of childbirth within hours. Actually one of the most powerful treatments for depression is electric shock, which destroys memories.

There is also the mystery of what memory and information you need to remember for survival. If you live to an age of seventy-five, you would have lived 2,366,820,000 seconds, but most of us select out about 60 seconds cumulatively to mark the pivotal parts of our lives and make sense of our history and behaviors. Would it make sense to remember each and every second?

The good news is that as a species we are getting smarter each decade, according to the researchers of intelligence using a limited test for measurement. But I wonder how we can measure up to the wisdom of our ancestors and their achievements in creating tremendous cultures. The Romans, Greeks, and Egyptians certainly were creators of amazing, plumbing systems, buildings, and roads, and their weapons were the products of genius. Our technology has developed so we can destroy more property and offer conveniences to more people, but we still follow the words of spirituality and religion from those great and inspired ancient minds as guides for our lives today.

The epilogue for this book is really a question: What are the boundaries of human intelligence, and specifically of yours? I really do not expect any answer because anytime you articulate a response, regardless of how reasonable or ridiculous it may be, it creates a boundary. You create your own limitations by pronouncing how far you will go.

When I coached track many years ago, the head coach was Max Goldsmith, who was a genius in his field. He took kids from a small west Texas town and continued to win the state championship year after year. He gave me several helpful suggestions, but the one that is relevant to all of life is this: If your goal is to run a 100-yard dash, do not train your athlete to run exactly 100 yards, teach him (or her) to run at least 110 yards. If you teach a kid to run just to his or her goal, that individual will stop at or before the finish line because this line was defined as the limit of their dream.

I am sure you read this book with a goal of some kind, and believe in goals as marks of success. This gives you confidence, especially if these objectives are reasonable for your progress; however, there is always another level to reach. This next limit may not be noted in the same measurement.

I am constantly impressed by people who perform amazing feats—they are always going forward in some direction in their lives. The contrasting example is the person who still sits in his chair and tries to recapture his high-school days in which he was the star. That person reached his goals and quit, and when you quit, your whole body and brain also quit.

According to Dr. Deborah Ruf, gifted children's coordinator of Mensa, there are ten characteristics of people who discover their gifts of intelligence and creativity:

1. Unique perceptions of the world with high levels of humor and generosity

2. High sensitivity to others

3. Intensity for altruistic missions

4. Multipotentiality for capabilities in many areas of interest

5. High striving for moral integrity

6. Lower sense of entitlement and high responsibility

7. High needs for self-actualization

8. Self-determination

9. High tendency to seek out injustice

10. Respect for all human beings

If you run down this list, do you not see why you would want this type of person living next to you? By bringing your brain into its maximum efficiency, you give a gift. Perhaps I am making this concept too simplistic, but I feel that it is an obligation to myself, to your family, to your God, and to you to honor your destiny for personal growth, especially cognitively. I have yet to meet a person who could not give me a gift of wisdom or information, and I would be less of myself if you were less of you. I believe that everyone has some destiny on this earth, whether it is being a hero or being in the audience to support someone else.

My first love in psychology was the rehabilitation specialty. I loved the courage of people who had major challenges in their lives to make their goals. They are my heroes because they enrich my life. Whether you have cancer, diabetes, depression, ADD, or any other challenge, you can create a story that will be a blessing to you as well as to the rest of us. You are more than a disease or disorder; you are a soul with amazing powers and strengths. Please do not hide behind your limitations.

The message is that these concepts and action steps I have presented in this book are to be used for more than the short-term goals of passing tests and achieving economic stardom. They are given for you to discover the authentic self and the precious soul within you. I wish I could tell you face-to-face how big a part you play in this story.

My dream would be to record every person's life and distill the wonderful and powerful stories each of us has to tell. It has been so discouraging that I never knew my great-grandfather who fought in the Civil War and later became a pastor, but he kept a journal with his stories of wisdom there. But I will never know why his daughter, who was a legend for her charitable work in the Eastern Star organization, committed suicide, or the story of why my great uncle was killed by the Ku Klux Klan before I was born. There are so many stories of great courage that we will never know.

Your life is important, and your growth into your authenticity will be exciting. Use these techniques to become everything positive you can be for yourself as well as for your family, because you are part of something greater than yourself. Your brain will expand to equip you to find your dreams and what you need to learn for joy and success. I promised you abundance with these skills, and you now have the tools to find that abundance regardless of how you define it.

As my father said to me, "Go and be the person God believed you would become."

AFTERWORD

As you read this book, some of Frank Lawlis's examples taken from his experience with his patients may have resonated with you. If you get only one thing from reading this book, it will be the sense of comfort that comes from knowing that you are not alone. Among the examples Dr. Lawlis mentions as advanced thinkers, several belong to or are involved with Mensa, the organization for the common person with an *un*common brain. In Mensa you are likely to find connections with people who have some of the same concerns, issues, limitations, and debilitations in addition to being intelligent.

Founded in England, Mensa began as a roundtable society in which those who belong meet only one qualification—scoring in the ninety-eighth percentile on a standardized IQ test. Today Mensa continues to expand around the world with more than 100,000 members in more than fifty countries.

As Mensa's supervisory psychologist, Dr. Lawlis works with our organization in evaluating the tests we use and other qualifications for membership. But even more than that, Dr. Lawlis works with us to help create awareness about intelligence—its gifts and challenges.

Today there is much written about emotional IQ (EQ), creativity IQ (CQ), and other dimensions of giftedness. While Mensa membership doesn't measure those areas, our members represent the full spectrum of dimensions of giftedness. When people ask what a typical Mensan is like, I often say that with members in the top 2 percent of intelligence, we have members who represent 2 percent of everything. Our members span every conceivable occupation, education level, background, and interest.

*   *   *

When Mensans are asked what motivates them to join, they give a variety of answers—often as varied as the members themselves—but they have a common theme. It is often to prove something to themselves, an ex-wife, boss, mother-in-law, or the fourth-grade teacher who said they would never amount to anything. In Mensa, people find peace of mind and a place where they can be themselves.

In addition to the intellect that helps them qualify for membership, another facet common to most Mensans is an awareness of being "different." Many of them have found that their minds aren't "wired" in the same way as other people's, and as a result, they sometimes feel out of sync with the world around them. In Mensa, they find others who are accepting and challenging, nurturing and supportive. Members frequently talk about the second family they find in the organization. Another comment I have heard many times is that Mensa is a place where you never have to explain your jokes.

Over the last six centuries, the organization has evolved from a handful of attorneys interested in the concept of nurturance of intelligence for humankind, to events and programs of all varieties and interests. Members range in age from four to more than one hundred. Our local groups (chapters) and special interest groups offer the added dimension of a membership within a membership. Not only does Mensa provide a way for you to gather with others who are as bright as you are, but you can find other bright people who share your unique interest, whether it's science, the arts, sports, or beyond.

Dr. Lawlis's book offers everyone—whether highly intelligent, slightly smarter than the average bear, or squarely in the middle—a way to evaluate whether your brain is working at its optimum, and, more important, the means to immediately start "training your brain" to work better, smarter, faster (without benefit of a $6 million transplant).

Pamela L. Donahoo, CAE
Executive Director
American Mensa Ltd.

RELAXATION SCRIPT FOR HIGHER COGNITIVE FUNCTIONING

The first requirement is for you to be in a place, both physically and psychologically, in which you can place your total attention on relaxation—no phone, no faxes, no outside interference to distract your focus. If there are things that happen, you can use those events to deepen your concentration of relaxing. Be sure you are in a posture in which you can let go of your tension without fear of falling or too much demand for gravity resistance.

Begin to focus on your breathing, not heavy breathing or regimented breathing, just becoming aware of the breathing cycle—in and out—in and out. All you have to do now is notice your breathing, being sure to breathe in through your nose and allowing the breath to leave your body whether through your nose or mouth. Just breathing in your natural way, no criticisms or defensiveness about your performance, just breathing and focusing on your breathing.

Now begin to allow the tension in your body to dissolve with your out-breath. Just allow the tension to go out through your out-breath, and as you feel the tension begin to leave, gently allow your eyes to close. Allow your breathing to do the relaxing and destressing for you. Try not to rush this, but allow enough time to pass so you can begin to feel relaxed.

Allow your body to relax more and more with each breath, always just focusing on your breath. If any thought or worry comes through your mind, just allow it to fly in and out through your breath and leave your mind. Spend some time just focusing on your breath and allowing your mind to go blank and erase all of your thoughts away.

Now focus on your feet and relax them through your breath. Cleanse your feet with the power of your out-breath, opening up the spaces between your joints, your bones, your muscles. Feel the warmth as the blood begins to circulate more freely, just focusing on your feet and breathing.

Now focus on the lower legs, your calf muscles, and relax these tissues. Breathe out the tension in your lower legs and relax deeper. Feel the blood flowing more and more easily through those lower leg muscles into your feet.

Now focus on your upper leg muscles, your thighs and hamstrings, gently relaxing them with your breath. Becoming more and more relaxed in all of your legs and helping the blood circulate and cleanse your leg muscles. Just breathing and relaxing.

Now focus on your hip muscles, your pelvis, and those organs tucked away in the cradle of your body. Breathe through this area and relax all of it. This is often the place where fear is based. If that is so, breathe away that emotion and replace it with security. If this is your way of dealing with stress, breathe away the stress in this area. Let a little out each time you breathe out.

Now focus on your chest. This is often the area of love and emotion. It is also the place we feel the most rejection and criticism. Breathe out those negative feelings and breathe in good feelings of self-care and nurturance. Breathing in and out, you can cleanse your heartfelt feelings about yourself. Breathe and feel better and better.

Now focus on your shoulders and arms. This is where you often build the most tension about responsibilities and demands. Breathe and relax those shoulder muscles and let go of the stress in your arms. Let go of the demands you put on yourself. Relax more and more in these areas. Now follow your body through your neck and into your head. Relax and breathe through the jaw muscles, relaxing them more and more. Tell yourself just to relax those muscles that you often use to stifle your anger and relax those muscles you hold when you are frightened. Relax with your breathing.

Now allow your whole body to begin to relax together. Breathe through your whole body, allowing it to feel like it is one feeling throughout. Breathe through your whole body, allowing every muscle to become more and more relaxed. If there is one part that is tense just focus on that part and breathe through it and relax.

Deeper and deeper into relaxation and letting things go. Just allow yourself to float and suspend your worries. Just keep focusing on the breathing. Relax . . . Relax . . . Relax . . .

INDEX